THE ALEXANDER SHAKESPEARE

General Editor
R. B. KENNEDY

The Tempest

PREFATORY NOTE

This series of Shakespeare's plays uses the full Alexander text which is recommended by many Examining Boards. By keeping in mind the fact that the language has changed considerably in four hundred years, as have customs, jokes, and stage conventions, the editors have aimed at helping the modern reader – whether English is his mother tongue or not – to grasp the full significance of these plays. The Notes, intended primarily for examination candidates, are presented in a simple, direct style. The needs of those unfamiliar with British culture have been specially considered.

Since quiet study of the printed word is unlikely to bring fully to life plays that were written directly for the public theatre, attention has been drawn to dramatic effects which are important in performance. The editors see Shakespeare's plays as living works of art which can be enjoyed today on stage, film and television in many parts of the world.

Contents

The Theatre in Shakespeare's Day	9
Shakespeare's Life and Times	15
Money in Shakespeare's Day	19
Introduction to the Play	21
Characters, Text and Notes	25
Summing Up	201
Appendix	209
Theme Index	213
Further Reading	215

An Elizabethan playhouse. Note the apron stage protruding into the auditorium, the space below it, the inner room at the rear of the stage, the gallery above the inner stage, the canopy over the main stage, and the absence of a roof over the audience.

THE THEATRE IN SHAKESPEARE'S DAY

On the face of it, the conditions in the Elizabethan theatre were not such as to encourage great writers. The public playhouse itself was not very different from an ordinary inn-yard; it was open to the weather; among the spectators were often louts, pickpockets and prostitutes; some of the actors played up to the rowdy elements in the audience by inserting their own jokes into the authors' lines, while others spoke their words loudly but unfeelingly; the presentation was often rough and noisy, with fireworks to represent storms and battles, and a table and a few chairs to represent a tavern; there were no actresses, so boys took the parts of women, even such subtle and mature ones as Cleopatra and Lady Macbeth; there was rarely any scenery at all in the modern sense. In fact, a quick inspection of the English theatre in the reign of Elizabeth I by a time-traveller from the twentieth century might well produce only one positive reaction: the costumes were often elaborate and beautiful.

Shakespeare himself makes frequent comments in his plays about the limitations of the playhouse and the actors of his time, often apologizing for them. At the beginning of *Henry V* the Prologue refers to the stage as 'this unworthy scaffold' and to the theatre building (the Globe, probably) as 'this wooden O', and emphasizes the urgent need for imagination in making up for all the deficiencies of presentation. In introducing Act IV the Chorus goes so far as to say:

> '... we shall much disgrace
> With four or five most vile and ragged foils,
> Right ill-dispos'd in brawl ridiculous,
> The name of Agincourt.'   (lines 49–52)

In *A Midsummer Night's Dream* (Act V, Scene i) he seems to dismiss actors with the words:

> 'The best in this kind are but shadows.'

Yet Elizabeth's theatre, with all its faults, stimulated dramatists to a variety of achievement that has never been equalled and, in Shakespeare, produced one of the greatest writers in history. In spite of all his grumbles he seems to have been fascinated by the challenge that it presented him with. It is necessary to re-examine his theatre carefully in order to understand how he was able to achieve so much with the materials he chose to use. What sort of place was the Elizabethan playhouse in reality? What sort of people were these criticized actors? And what sort of audiences gave them their living.

The Development of the Theatre up to Shakespeare's Time

For centuries in England noblemen had employed groups of skilled people to entertain them when required. Under Tudor rule, as England became more secure and united, actors such as these were given more freedom, and they often performed in public, while still acknowledging their 'overlords' (in the 1570s, for example, when Shakespeare was still a schoolboy at Stratford, one famous company was called 'Lord Leicester's Men'). London was rapidly becoming larger and more important in the second half of the sixteenth century, and many of the companies of actors took the opportunities offered to establish themselves at inns on the main roads leading to the City (for example, the Boar's Head in Whitechapel and the Tabard in Southwark) or in the City itself. These groups of actors would come to an agreement with the inn-keeper which would give them the use of the yard for their performances after people had eaten and drunk well in the middle of the day. Before long, some inns were taken over completely by companies of players and thus became the first public theatres. In 1574 the officials of the City of London issued an order which shows clearly that these theatres were both popular and also offensive to some respectable people, because the order complains about 'the inordinate haunting of great multitudes of people, specially youth, to plays interludes and shows; namely occasion of frays and quarrels, evil practices of incontinency in great inns …' There is evidence that, on public holidays, the theatres on the banks of the Thames were crowded with noisy apprentices and tradesmen, but it would be wrong to think that audiences were always undiscriminating and loud-mouthed. In spite of the disapproval of Puritans and the more staid members of society, by the 1590s, when Shakespeare's plays were beginning to be performed, audiences consisted of a good cross-section of English society, nobility as well as workers, intellectuals as well as simple people out for a laugh; also (and in this respect English theatres were unique in Europe), it was quite normal for respectable women to attend plays. So Shakespeare had to write plays which would appeal to people of widely different kinds. He had to provide 'something for everyone' but at the same time to take care to unify the material so that it would not seem to fall into separate pieces as they watched it. A speech like that of the drunken porter in *Macbeth* could provide the 'groundlings' with a belly-laugh, but also held a deeper significance for those who could appreciate it. The audience he wrote for was one of a number of apparent drawbacks which Shakespeare was able to turn to his and our advantage.

Shakespeare's Actors

Nor were all the actors of the time mere 'rogues, vagabonds and sturdy beggars' as some were described in a Statute of 1572. It is true that many of them had a hard life and earned very little money, but leading actors could become partners in the ownership of the theatres in which they acted: Shakespeare was a shareholder in the Globe and the Blackfriars theatres when he was an actor as well as a playwright. In any case, the attacks made on Elizabethan actors were usually directed at their morals and not at their acting ability; it is clear that many of them must have been good at their trade if they were able to interpret complex works like the great tragedies in such a way as to attract enthusiastic audiences. Undoubtedly some of the boys took the women's parts with skill and confidence, since a man called Coryate, visiting Venice in 1611, expressed surprise that women could act as well as they: 'I saw women act, a thing that I never saw before ... and they performed it with as good a grace, action, gesture ... as ever I saw any masculine actor.' The quality of most of the actors who first presented Shakespeare's plays is probably accurately summed up by Fynes Moryson, who wrote, '... as there be, in my opinion, more plays in London than in all the parts of the world I have seen, so do these players or comedians excel all other in the world.'

The Structure of the Public Theatre

Although the 'purpose-built' theatres were based on the inn-yards which had been used for play-acting, most of them were circular. The walls contained galleries on three storeys from which the wealthier patrons watched; they must have been something like the 'boxes' in a modern theatre, except that they held much larger numbers – as many as 1500. The 'groundlings' stood on the floor of the building, facing a raised stage which projected from the 'stage-wall', the main features of which were:

1. a small room opening on to the back of the main stage and on the same level as it (rear stage);
2. a gallery above this inner stage (upper stage);
3. a canopy projecting from above the gallery over the main stage, to protect the actors from the weather (the 700 or 800 members of the audience who occupied the yard, or 'pit' as we call it today, had the sky above them).

In addition to these features there were dressing-rooms behind the stage and a space underneath it from which entrances could be made through trap-doors. All the acting areas – main stage, rear stage, upper stage and under stage – could be entered by actors directly from their dressing rooms, and all of them were used in productions of Shakespeare's plays. For example, the inner stage, an almost cave-like structure, would have been where Ferdinand and Miranda are 'discovered' playing chess in the last act of *The Tempest*, while the upper stage was certainly the balcony from which Romeo climbs down in Act III of *Romeo and Juliet*.

It can be seen that such a building, simple but adaptable, was not really unsuited to the presentation of plays like Shakespeare's. On the contrary, its simplicity guaranteed the minimum of distraction, while its shape and construction must have produced a sense of involvement on the part of the audience that modern producers would envy.

Other Resources of the Elizabethan Theatre

Although there were few attempts at scenery in the public theatre (painted backcloths were occasionally used in court performances), Shakespeare and his fellow playwrights were able to make use of a fair variety of 'properties'; lists of such articles have survived: they include beds, tables, thrones, and also trees, walls, a gallows, a Trojan horse and a 'Mouth of Hell'; in a list of properties belonging to the manager, Philip Henslowe, the curious item 'two mossy banks' appears. Possibly one of them was used for the

> 'bank whereon the wild thyme blows,
> Where oxlips and the nodding violet grows'

in *A Midsummer Night's Dream* (Act II, Scene i). Once again, imagination must have been required of the audience.

Costumes were the one aspect of stage production in which trouble and expense were hardly ever spared to obtain a magnificent effect. Only occasionally did they attempt any historical accuracy (almost all Elizabethan productions were what we should call 'modern-dress' ones), but they were appropriate to the characters who wore them: kings were seen to be kings and beggars were similarly unmistakable. It is an odd fact that there was usually no attempt at illusion in the costuming: if a costume *looked* fine and rich it probably *was*. Indeed, some of the costumes were almost unbelievably expensive. Henslowe lent his company £19 to buy a cloak, and the Alleyn brothers, well-known actors, gave £20 for a 'black velvet cloak, with sleeves embroidered all with silver and gold, lined with black satin striped with gold'.

With the one exception of the costumes, the 'machinery' of the playhouse was economical and uncomplicated rather than crude and rough, as we can see from this second and more leisurely look at it. This meant that playwrights were stimulated to produce the imaginative effects that they wanted from the language that they used. In the case of a really great writer like Shakespeare, when he had learned his trade in the theatre as an actor, it seems that he received quite enough assistance of a mechanical and structural kind without having irksome restrictions and conventions imposed on him; it is interesting to try to guess what he would have done with the highly complex apparatus of a modern television studio. We can see when we look back to his time that he used his instrument, the Elizabethan theatre, to the full, but placed his ultimate reliance on the communication between his imagination and that of his audience through the medium of words. It is, above all, his rich and wonderful use of language that must have made play-going at that time a memorable experience for people of widely different kinds. Fortunately, the deep satisfaction of appreciating and enjoying Shakespeare's work can be ours also, if we are willing to overcome the language difficulty produced by the passing of time.

SHAKESPEARE'S LIFE AND TIMES

Very little indeed is known about Shakespeare's private life: the facts included here are almost the only indisputable ones. The dates of Shakespeare's plays are those on which they were first produced.

★ ★ ★

1558 Queen Elizabeth crowned.

1561 Francis Bacon born.

1564 Christopher Marlowe born.

William Shakespeare born, April 23rd, baptized April 26th.

1566

Shakespeare's brother, Gilbert, born.

1567 Mary, Queen of Scots, deposed.
James VI (later James I of England) crowned King of Scotland.

1572 Ben Jonson born.
Lord Leicester's Company (of players) licensed; later called Lord Strange's, then the Lord Chamberlain's and finally (under James) the King's Men.

1573 John Donne born.

1574 The Common Council of London directs that all plays and playhouses in London must be licensed.

1576 James Burbage builds the first public playhouse, The Theatre, at Shoreditch, outside the walls of the City.

1577 Francis Drake begins his voyage round the world (completed 1580).
Holinshed's *Chronicles of England, Scotland and Ireland* published (which Shakespeare later used extensively).

1582

Shakespeare married to Anne Hathaway.

1583 The Queen's Company founded by royal warrant.

Shakespeare's daughter, Susanna, born.

1585

Shakespeare's twins, Hamnet and Judith, born.

1586 Sir Philip Sidney, the Elizabethan ideal 'Christian knight', poet, patron, soldier, killed at Zutphen in the Low Countries.

1587 Mary, Queen of Scots, beheaded.
Marlowe's *Tamburlaine (Part I)* first staged.

1588 Defeat of the Spanish Armada.
Marlowe's *Tamburlaine (Part II)* first staged.

1589 Marlowe's *Jew of Malta* and Kyd's *Spanish Tragedy* (a 'revenge tragedy' and one of the most popular plays of Elizabethan times).

1590 Spenser's *Faerie Queene* (Books I–III) published.

1592 Marlowe's *Doctor Faustus* and *Edward II* first staged.
Witchcraft trials in Scotland.
Robert Greene, a rival playwright, refers to Shakespeare as 'an upstart crow' and 'the only Shake-scene in a country'.

Titus Andronicus
Henry VI, Parts I, II and III
Richard III

1593 London theatres closed by the plague.
Christopher Marlowe killed in a Deptford tavern.

Two Gentlemen of Verona
Comedy of Errors
The Taming of the Shrew
Love's Labour's Lost

1594 Shakespeare's company becomes The Lord Chamberlain's Men.

Romeo and Juliet

1595 Raleigh's first expedition to Guiana. Last expedition of Drake and Hawkins (both died).

Richard II
A Midsummer Night's Dream

1596 Spenser's *Faerie Queene* (Books IV–VI) published.
James Burbage buys rooms at Blackfriars and begins to convert them into a theatre.

King John
The Merchant of Venice
Shakespeare's son Hamnet dies.
Shakespeare's father is granted a coat of arms.

1597	James Burbage dies, his son Richard, a famous actor, turns the Blackfriars Theatre into a private playhouse.	*Henry IV (Part I)* Shakespeare buys and redecorates New Place at Stratford.
1598	Death of Philip II of Spain	*Henry IV (Part II)* *Much Ado About Nothing*
1599	Death of Edmund Spenser. The Globe Theatre completed at Bankside by Richard and Cuthbert Burbage.	*Henry V* *Julius Caesar* *As You Like It*
1600	Fortune Theatre built at Cripplegate. East India Company founded for the extension of English trade and influence in the East. The Children of the Chapel begin to use the hall at Blackfriars.	*Merry Wives of Windsor* *Troilus and Cressida*
1601		*Hamlet*
1602	Sir Thomas Bodley's library opened at Oxford.	*Twelfth Night*
1603	Death of Queen Elizabeth. James I comes to the throne. Shakespeare's company becomes The King's Men. Raleigh tried, condemned and sent to the Tower	
1604	Treaty of peace with Spain	*Measure for Measure* *Othello* *All's Well that Ends Well*
1605	The Gunpowder Plot: an attempt by a group of Catholics to blow up the Houses of Parliament.	
1606	Guy Fawkes and other plotters executed.	*Macbeth* *King Lear*
1607	Virginia, in America, colonized. A great frost in England.	*Antony and Cleopatra* *Timon of Athens* *Coriolanus* Shakespeare's daughter, Susanna, married to Dr. John Hall.

1608 The company of the Children of the Chapel Royal (who had performed at Blackfriars for ten years) is disbanded.
John Milton born.
Notorious pirates executed in London.

Richard Burbage leases the Blackfriars Theatre to six of his fellow actors, including Shakespeare.
Pericles, Prince of Tyre

1609

Shakespeare's *Sonnets* published.

1610 A great drought in England

Cymbeline

1611 Chapman completes his great translation of the *Iliad*, the story of Troy.
Authorized Version of the Bible published.

A Winter's Tale
The Tempest

1612 Webster's *The White Devil* first staged.

Shakespeare's brother, Gilbert, dies.

1613 Globe theatre burnt down during a performance of *Henry VIII* (the firing of small cannon set fire to the thatched roof).
Webster's *Duchess of Malfi* first staged.

Henry VIII
Two Noble Kinsmen
Shakespeare buys a house at Blackfriars.

1614 Globe Theatre rebuilt 'in far finer manner than before'.

1616 Ben Jonson publishes his plays in one volume.
Raleigh released from the Tower in order to prepare an expedition to the gold mines of Guiana.

Shakespeare's daughter, Judith, marries Thomas Quiney.
Death of Shakespeare on his birthday, April 23rd.

1618 Raleigh returns to England and is executed on the charge for which he was imprisoned in 1603.

1623 Publication of the Folio edition of Shakespeare's plays

Death of Anne Shakespeare (née Hathaway).

MONEY IN SHAKESPEARE'S DAY

It is extremely difficult, if not impossible, to relate the value of money in our time to its value in another age and to compare prices of commodities today and in the past. Many items are simply not comparable on grounds of quality or serviceability.

There was a bewildering variety of coins in use in Elizabethan England. As nearly all English and European coins were gold or silver, they had intrinsic value apart from their official value. This meant that foreign coins circulated freely in England and were officially recognized, for example the French crown (écu) worth about 30p (72 cents), and the Spanish ducat worth about 33p (79 cents). The following table shows some of the coins mentioned by Shakespeare and their relation to one another.

GOLD	British	American	SILVER	British	American
sovereign (heavy type)	£1.50	$3.60	shilling	10p	24c
sovereign (light type)	66p–£1	$1.58–$2.40	groat	1.5p	4c
angel	33p–50p	79c–$1.20			
royal	50p	$1.20			
noble	33p	79c			
crown	25p	60c			

A comparison of the following prices in Shakespeare's time with the prices of the same items today will give some idea of the change in the value of money.

ITEM	PRICE British	American	ITEM	PRICE British	American
beef, per lb.	0.5p	1c	cherries (lb.)	1p	2c
mutton, leg	7.5p	18c	7 oranges	1p	2c
rabbit	3.5p	9c	1 lemon	1p	2c
chicken	3p	8c	cream (quart)	2.5p	6c
potatoes (lb)	10p	24c	sugar (lb.)	£1	$2.40
carrots (bnch)	1p	2c	sack (wine) (gal.)	14p	34c
8 artichokes	4p	9c	tobacco (oz.)	25p	60c
1 cucumber	1p	2c	biscuits (lb.)	12.5p	30c

INTRODUCTION

The Tempest, like any work of art, was partly conditioned by the times and circumstances in which it was created. It was written at the end of Shakespeare's career in the theatre and contains many of the themes which appear in his earlier plays. Nevertheless it shows new features and fresh experimentation with dramatic forms. Writers have suggested that in the epilogue he is bidding farewell to the stage before retiring to Stratford, and this may be so. It is certainly tempting to see in the magician Prospero the artist Shakespeare. But whether or not we think that there are autobiographical references in the play, it may be useful to try to look over Shakespeare's shoulder as he begins this play and so increase our understanding of what *The Tempest* is about.

We can start with its title. In 1609 nine ships were on their way from England carrying five hundred colonists to Virginia when a hurricane hit the little fleet; the flagship *Sea Adventure* was wrecked off the Bermudas but the passengers and crew miraculously managed to get ashore safely. They rebuilt the ship and reached their destination the following year. The contemporary account by Strachey (see Appendix) almost certainly set Shakespeare's mind working. In the early 17th century the New World of the American continent was exciting men's imaginations as vividly as space exploration excites our imaginations today – and perhaps even more hopefully. Here perhaps lay a chance for men to make a fresh start, to leave behind a bad old past. The ideas of discovery and of self-discovery are central to the play.

If Strachey's account stimulated Shakespeare's first ideas for the play, a contemporary theatrical fashion influenced him in many of its features. This was the Masque, an indoor fantasy-entertainment which had developed at the Court and in private theatres and which contrasted quite sharply with the more realistic drama of the public theatres. Plot characterization and dialogue were less important than spectacular scenery, splendid costumes, musical effects, songs, dancing, and stately verse. A rough comparison might be made between straight drama and opera or ballet in the theatre today. The masque was an aristocratic and artificial form of drama in which the ideal was more important than the real, ideas than characters. It often celebrated a special occasion, such as a royal wedding. Not only does *The Tempest* contain a mini-masque (to celebrate the betrothal of the royal lovers in the play) but it is often masque-like in itself, with its spectacular storm-scene, supernatural music, magician's banquet, and exotic characters such as the spirit Ariel and the grotesque savage Caliban. Masques make a strong appeal to eyes and ears, and this is more obviously true of *The Tempest* than of any other Shakespeare play.

The masque-influence in the play extends to the characters and to the setting. It would certainly not be true to say that the characters are lacking in reality and are simply two-dimensional 'types' or flat caricatures; much of the verse dialogue is as natural as everyday speech and there is a dramatic narrative within which they can develop. But the play is a very short one (about half the length of *Hamlet*, for instance) and its compression does cramp characterization. Perhaps this was Shakespeare's deliberate intention at the outset: this was to be a play in which themes were to be more important than characters, and *kinds* of people were to be shown rather than individuals.

The setting contributes to the 'distancing' effect of the masque, as if we were on a different plane of existence while watching the play. At the beginning and end of *The Tempest* it is true that we are in the real world of ships and simple mariners, but on the island itself we are in the realm of fantasy, though that dream-world has the vividness and clarity of a dream which seems more real than the existence to which we return when we wake up – or leave the theatre. This feeling of being in a dream is contributed to by the number of references to sleep and waking there are in the play.

The Tempest is not only a very short play but it is one of Shakespeare's most neatly organized. Whereas the action in his other plays spreads and sprawls like life itself over a period of time, this is constructed, like classical drama, within the tight framework of the 'unities' of time, place and action (the plot and characters). The events on the island take place in the afternoon between two and six o'clock, 'stage-time' and 'audience-time' being almost identical. Once on the island the characters remain there throughout the play and are therefore in a sense in one place. And although there are three 'plots' developing simultaneously, they are moving to a common conclusion, and with a strong feeling of unity, under Prospero's control.

An interesting effect of this compression is to emphasize the importance of time in the play: the events which precede the play and are only referred to – the usurpation of Prospero by his brother Antonio in far-off Milan twelve long years ago; the wedding of Claribel in distant Tunis from which Alonso's court are returning to Naples – these are made to seem remote in time and space. Just as the island, like any island, appears even more detached from the world than it actually is, so has time seemed on the island. But suddenly destiny has brought together those who thought that the past was dead; those great distances of time and space had shrunk to the size of a small island and the urgency of a few hours.

What is *The Tempest* 'about'. The Summing-up will suggest some thoughts about the characters and the themes which they develop, in answering this question; and in an Introduction only a few broad hints are required. It has already been suggested that the play is about discovery and self-discovery: those who come to Prospero's island, like the lovers who come to the wood near Athens in that other dream-play, *A Midsummer Night's Dream*, make discoveries about each other and about themselves which change their lives. Even the 'presiding deity' of the island, Prospero himself, makes discoveries. Magician he may be, but he is also a developing human being. It is a play about metamorphosis or change, about how our lives can be dramatically transformed, for example when we suddenly and it seems miraculously fall in love, or when a truth is suddenly revealed to our understanding. It is a play about being imprisoned, not only physically but within the limitations of our understanding, or of our own natures, and about being released from that bondage. It is about the need for self-control and the discipline of education if we are to become masters of any art or science, masters of other people, or (above all) masters of ourselves. These themes insistently weave their way to and fro through the language and imagery of a play in which the sense of revelation is perhaps the key emotion. If the play expresses a single feeling, it is 'How strange life is! And how wonderful.'

LIST OF CHARACTERS

ALONSO	*King of Naples*
SEBASTIAN	*his brother*
PROSPERO	*the right Duke of Milan*
ANTONIO	*his brother, the usurping Duke of Milan*
FERDINAND	*son to the King of Naples*
GONZALO	*an honest old counsellor*
ADRIAN	*Lords*
FRANCISCO	
CALIBAN	*a savage and deformed slave*
TRINCULO	*a jester*
STEPHANO	*a drunken butler*
MASTER OF A SHIP	
BOATSWAIN	
MARINERS	
MIRANDA	*daughter to Prospero*
ARIEL	*an airy spirit*
IRIS	
CERES	
JUNO	*spirits*
NYMPHS	
REAPERS	
OTHER SPIRITS	*attending on Prospero*

THE SCENE: *A ship at sea; afterwards an uninhabited island*

The first scene of the play, the only one not to take place on the island itself, opens the action with vivid realism and, for the seafarers in Shakespeare's audience, the familiar violence of wind and waves. The sound of thunder, created by rolling a cannonball in a wooden barrel off-stage, and the flashes of lightning produced by gunpowder, plunge the audience into the play without any preamble. The projecting stage becomes in the lurching movements of the actors a rolling main deck, and the upper stage or balcony the poop deck. It is a scene of mounting panic and confusion in which, although we are given brief impressions of the characters of the king and his court by their reactions to danger, we are not told their names.

The Shipmaster is the Captain of the vessel, and the Boatswain is his chief asssistant. They probably enter respectively on the upper and lower stage levels, the Master shouting from the poop deck to the Boatswain on the main deck or 'waist'.

2. what cheer? how goes it?

3. Good! either 'Fine!' or simply returning the greeting as present-day naval officers do by saying 'Very good!' or possibly an encouraging, 'Good Fellow', (compare lines 15 and 18).

3. fall to't yarely 'get cracking!' or 'jump to it.'

3. yarely nimbly, briskly.

4–5. * bestir ... yare the urgency of these repetitions is further emphasized by the short, sharp, imperative sentences in which much of the scene is expressed. The Boatswain follows the Master's lead and mixes encouraging phrases with crisp commands.

4–5. bestir look lively! Move!

6. * Take ... topsail i.e. to prevent the ship being blown further in towards the shore.

6. Tend to pay attention to.

6. master's whistle used only by the Master, to control his crew's management of the ship. Like a bugle-note above the noise of battle, his whiste could be heard in any storm.

7–8. * Blow ... enough perhaps the whistle has just blown, and the Boatswain then shouts at the storm to burst its lungs with blowing, provided that the ship has sufficient sea-room in which to manoeuvre.

Stage Direction. **Enter Alonso etc.** their fine court robes, which when we see them next are, by means of Prospero's magical power, as fresh as new despite being soaked in the sea, distinguish them clearly from the mariners, just as their ineffective landlubberly movements contrast with the businesslike actions of the crew.

10. Play the men Alonso either means, 'Behave like men', or he is urging the busy Boatswain to 'Play the men' i.e. work them hard, unnecessary advice in the circumstances.

THE SCENE: A SHIP AT SEA; AFTERWARDS
AN UNINHABITED ISLAND

ACT ONE

SCENE I. – On a ship at sea; a tempestuous noise of thunder and lightning heard.

[Enter a SHIPMASTER and a BOATSWAIN]

Shipmaster
  Boatswain!
Boatswain
  Here, master; what cheer?
Shipmaster
  Good! Speak to th' mariners; fall to 't yarely, or we
  run ourselves aground; bestir, bestir.

[Exit]

[Enter MARINERS]

Boatswain
  Heigh, my hearts! cheerly, cheerly, my hearts! yare,   5
  yare! Take in the topsail. Tend to th' master's
  whistle. Blow till thou burst thy wind, if room
  enough.

[Enter ALONSO, SEBASTIAN, ANTONIO, FERDINAND,
GONZALO and OTHERS]

Alonso
  Good boatswain, have care. Where's the master?
  Play the men.   10
Boatswain
  I pray now, keep below.
Antonio
  Where is the master, boson?

13. * Do … him? can't you hear his whistle?

13. * You … labour you are spoiling our efforts. (i.e. We can't do our job if you keep getting in the way.)

15. * Nay … patient Gonzalo's role in life is to be diplomatic, as Alonso's chief counsellor: he is himself an example of patient cheerfulness in adversity throughout the play.

16–17. * What … king? the use of a singular verb with a plural subject was quite common at the time.

16–17. roarers not only expresses the sound of the waves raging but may also suggest the 'roaring boys' or 'young rogues', rebellious gallants at court: Alonso is being threatened by the waves, as is his corrupt court.

18. * whom … aboard i.e. the king, therefore take extra care.

19. * You … counsellor Gonzalo is a 'counsellor' in that he gives advice, but he is also a 'councillor', a member of Alonso's Privy Council, with powers to keep civil order in the kingdom. He is however powerless to command *these* elements.

21–2. present present moment.

21–2. hand handle

23–4. * make … ready prepare yourself by prayer (for the next world, if need be).

23–4. * mischance … hour misfortune that may occur at any moment.

27. comfort consolation, reassurance.

28–9. drowning-mark birth-mark or mole on his body to predict that he will die by drowning. (Such moles or marks were superstitiously supposed to indicate how a man would die.)

28–9. perfect gallows i.e. is a sure sign that he will be hanged rather than die in any other way. (This refers to the proverb that he that is born to be hanged will never be drowned.)

28–9. complexion (a) facial appearance, (b) temperament (as determined by astrological influences at his birth which gave his character a certain 'make-up').

29–31. * Stand … advantage Stick to your word, dear Mistress Fortune, that the Boatswain is going to be hanged, and see to it that the rope from which he is destined to swing is our lifeline, since our own is not much use in this storm.

29–31. cable anchor rope.

32. * our … miserable our position is wretched, hopeless.

33. * Down … topmast the topsail has already been taken down after being furled, and the next step is to lower the topmast. (In this and the other details of handling a ship in a storm Shakespeare shows precise, though not necessarily first-hand, knowledge of 17th-century seamanship.)

33–4. * Bring … maincourse the dangerous movement towards the shore has been partially checked by lowering the topsail and topmast; now the Boatswain attempts to heave-to (**try**) by using the mainsail (**maincourse**) to control the drift.

35–6. * louder … office the passengers' cries are louder than the tempest or our shouts as we work the ship.

Boatswain

Do you not hear him? You mar our labour; keep
your cabins; you do assist the storm.

Gonzalo

Nay, good, be patient.   15

Boatswain

When the sea is. Hence! What cares these roarers for
the name of king? To cabin! silence! Trouble us not.

Gonzalo

Good, yet remember whom thou hast aboard.

Boatswain

None that I more love than myself. You are a
counsellor; if you can command these elements to   20
silence, and work the peace of the present, we will
not hand a rope more. Use your authority; if you
cannot, give thanks you have liv'd so long, and
make yourself ready in your cabin for the
mischance of the hour, if it so hap. – Cheerly, good   25
hearts! – Out of our way, I say.

[Exit]

Gonzalo

I have great comfort from this fellow. Methinks he
hath no drowning mark upon him; his complexion
is perfect gallows. Stand fast, good Fate, to his
hanging; make the rope of his destiny our cable, for   30
our own doth little advantage. If he be not born to
be hang'd, our case is miserable.

[Exeunt]

[Re-enter BOATSWAIN]

Boatswain

Down with the topmast. Yare, lower, lower! Bring
her to try wi' th' maincourse. [A cry within] A
plague upon this howling! They are louder than the   35
weather or our office.

37. give o'er give up, stop working.

42. whoreson filthy, despicable (lit. 'You bastard', i.e. son of a whore, prostitute).

45. * **I'll … drowning** I guarantee he won't drown.

46–7. * **as … wench** possibly 'As open (accessible) as a whore.' If so, it seems a crude simile to come from Gonzalo's lips, though not from Sebastian's or Antonio's, perhaps.

48–9. * **Lay … a-hold** i.e. heave-to, bring her bows into the wind to prevent any further movement towards the dangerously close shore.

48–9. set her two courses set the ship's foresail and mainsail. (This last, desperate measure is to get the ship moving again under sail by setting the large sails to use the wind against itself, i.e. at such an angle that the vessel tacks away from the shore instead of being blown on to it.)

48–9. off to sea again i.e. instead of getting any further inshore.

51. * **What … cold?** 'A cold mouth' is an image of death, but the Boatswain may be taking a final swig from his flask to keep himself warm when he is plunged into the cold sea, or taking a last leave of the crew, drinking to each other.

52. Prince i.e. Ferdinand.

53. assist attend, wait upon. (Even in the dangerous situation of the shipwreck, Gonzalo remains the loyal counsellor, whose place is at the King's side.)

52–64. * Verse follows the prose used by the working men, to distinguish the courtiers, though it is ironical that the apparently more dignified Sebastian and Antonio (in their speech and costume) should be more abusive and behave less well than their inferiors.

54. out of patience in direct contrast to the patient Gonzalo, who behaves with forebearance and Christian fortitude in the face of disaster.

55. merely entirely, completely.

56. wide-chopp'd open-mouthed, wide-jawed (partly because he has been drinking, and partly because he has been both shouting orders and answering back the nobles).

[Re-enter SEBASTIAN, ANTONIO, and GONZALO]

Yet again! What do you here? Shall we give o'er,
and drown? Have you a mind to sink?

Sebastian

A pox o' your throat, you bawling, blasphemous,
incharitable dog!   40

Boatswain

Work you, then.

Antonio

Hang, cur; hang, you whoreson, insolent noise-
maker; we are less afraid to be drown'd than thou
art.

Gonzalo

I'll warrant him for drowning, though the ship were   45
no stronger than a nutshell, and as leaky as an
unstanched wench.

Boatswain

Lay her a-hold, a-hold; set her two courses; off to
sea again; lay her off.

[Enter MARINERS, wet]

Mariners

All lost! to prayers, to prayers! all lost!   50

[Exeunt]

Boatswain

What, must our mouths be cold?

Gonzalo

The King and Prince at prayers! Let's assist them,
For our case is as theirs.

Sebastian   I am out of patience.

Antonio

We are merely cheated of our lives by drunkards.   55
This wide-chopp'd rascal – would thou mightst lie
    drowning

31

57. ten tides pirates were hanged at low-water mark and left there until three tides had washed over them. The emphasis given by alliteration and by stressing *ten* would show Antonio's bitter desperation. He and the others may, after all, soon be washed by many more than ten tides.

58–9. * Though ... glut the sound of these lines creates the suck and gurgle of the engulfing sea. (Perhaps there is a suggestion of Jonah and the Whale in line 59: and like Jonah the courtiers are to be regurgitated.)

58–9. swear against i.e. every soldier (*drop*) in Neptune's army takes an oath not to allow him to escape to be hanged rather than drowned.

58–9. at wid'st as widely as possible.

58–9. glut swallow.

62. We split the ship's breaking up!

62. wife and children i.e. the family left at home (compare Act II, Scene i, lines 4 and 129).

63–4. * King ... him although Alonso has spoken only once, and been seen only briefly, we are continually being reminded of his presence on board. As father of Ferdinand and also the means by which Antonio usurped the Dukedom from Prospero, he is the central figure of Prospero's revenge and reconciliation.

65–8. * Now ... death Gonzalo would willingly exchange any amount of sea for one acre of unproductive heathland. This reference to dry land not only prepares us for the next scene (though providentially the island is not wholly barren but partially fertile) but also increases our feeling that the stage is a ship at sea.

65–8. furze gorse, whin.

67–8. * The wills ... death Gonzalo, while submitting with Christian patience and humility to the wishes of the heavenly powers, would nevertheless prefer not to die by drowning. (It has been suggested that Gonzalo may be punning on a *dry death* i.e. one which evokes no tears for the departed. Throughout the scene Gonzalo has been distinguished by his spirited wit in the face of disaster.)

This opening scene, a prologue to the play, not only expresses the play's title in visual form and introduces the audience to some of the characters (though allowing us only to catch revealing glimpses of them, as if it were in flashes of lightning), but also establishes the idea of chaos and disorder in the human world, which Prospero by raising the tempest is both to use and control and in time (in the highly compressed action of the play) to turn, if only temporarily, to calm.

SCENE II

The first scene, one of confusion, is designed to make the audience ask questions: Who are these people? Where is the ship? Why the tempest and the apparent tragedy? The second scene, a long one, contrasts sharply with its short predecessor. It answers questions, presents its characters in 'close-up' detail, and introduces the setting of the play and its central situation.

It is divided into four phases, in each of which there is a similar though not

The washing of ten tides!
Gonzalo

                He'll be hang'd yet,
Though every drop of water swear against it,
And gape at wid'st to glut him.
[A confused noise within: 'Mercy on us!' –   60
'We split, we split!' – 'Farewell, my wife and
      children!' –
'Farewell, brother!' – 'We split, we split, we split!']
Antonio

Let's all sink wi' th' King.
Sebastian

Let's take leave of him.

      [Exeunt ANTONIO and SEBASTIAN]

Gonzalo

Now would I give a thousand furlongs of sea for an   65
acre of barren ground – long heath, brown furze,
any thing. The wills above be done, but I would fain
die a dry death.

          [Exeunt]

identical pattern, the elements of which are the references to past present, and future. Thus in phase one (lines 1–86), in speaking to Miranda, Prospero relates the present shipwreck to past events and hints at future opportunities; in phase two (lines 187–304), Ariel's demands to be released as a reward for his services in the tempest lead Prospero to remind him of his past and to promise him freedom in the near future; in phase three (lines 305–74), Caliban's present slavery makes him protest against Prospero's previous usurpation of the island, and provokes his master to threaten future punishment; and in phase four (lines 375–501), there are references to Ferdinand's Neapolitan past, though the emphasis is on the present and future with Miranda.

The broad movement of the scene, and of each of its phases, resembling that of the play itself, is from despair to hope, from imprisonment to release, from death to life.

Stage Direction. *Before … cell*: in the public playhouse the cell would probably be curtained 'discovery space' below the upper stage or balcony; at an indoor performance, it might be a cavelike construction on the rear raised stage.

cell: i.e. secluded home in a cave.

1. **art** magic. In lines 1 and 2 Miranda makes clear to the audience who Prospero is (her father), what he is (a magician), and how the tempest arose (by his magic power).

2. * **wild … roar** i.e. roused them to roaring like wild beasts (compare Act II, Scene i, line 307).

2. allay calm, soothe. Perhaps storm sounds should continue intermittently throughout this scene: thunder mutters in Act II, Scene ii, and is used by Ariel in Act III, Scene iii. Sound of all kinds, human, natural, supernatural, are essential to the particular atmosphere of the play, and especially in contrasting the evil and discordant with the good and harmonious.

3–5. * Miranda's description of the storm pictures a war between sea and sky (compare Act V, Scene i, lines 43–4). Hot, black tar (*stinking pitch*) is about to be poured down like boiling oil from the castle walls of the sky on to the attacking waves below when the mountainous sea rises to swamp it. The *welkin* (sky) is also thought of as having a *cheek*, i.e. the side of a grate of a fire or furnace, though *cheek* might also suggest cloud. (The image of siege recurs in line 205.)

5–6. * Miranda's *very virtue of compassion*, the keynote of her character, is shown here, reinforced by the repetition, *suffered, suffer,* and reiterated in lines 5 and 6.

6. brave fine, splendid. The sense of wonder and delight is great in this play. *Brave* occurs thirteen times, *bravely*, three times, and *braver*, once.

7. * Doubly ironical: Miranda does not know (a) that the ship has a king and his nobles on board, and (b) that the king and some of his court are ignoble.

8. the cry i.e. *we split, we split:* it knocked on the door of her heart.

13. fraughting souls cargo or freight of passengers and crew.

13. Be collected calm yourself, pull yourself together.

1–13. * All four elements of matter – earth, water, air and fire – are mentioned, Prospero commands the elements through the agency of his spirits, and the supremacy over the physical is a major theme.

SCENE II. The island. Before Prospero's cell.

[Enter PROSPERO and MIRANDA]

Miranda
    If by your art, my dearest father, you have
    Put the wild waters in this roar, allay them.
    The sky, it seems, would pour down stinking pitch,
    But that the sea, mounting to th' welkin's cheek,
    Dashes the fire out. O, I have suffered   5
    With those that I saw suffer! A brave vessel,
    Who had no doubt some noble creature in her,
    Dash'd all to pieces! O, the cry did knock
    Against my very heart! Poor souls, they perish'd.
    Had I been any god of power, I would   10
    Have sunk the sea within the earth or ere
    It should the good ship so have swallow'd and
    The fraughting souls within her.
Prospero   Be collected;
    No more amazement; tell your piteous heart
    There's no harm done.
Miranda   O, woe the day!
Prospero   No harm.   15
    I have done nothing but in care of thee,
    Of thee, my dear one, thee, my daughter, who
    Art ignorant of what thou art, nought knowing
    Of whence I am, nor that I am more better
    Than Prospero, master of a full poor cell,   20
    And thy no greater father.
Miranda   More to know
    Did never meddle with my thoughts.
Prospero   'Tis time
    I should inform thee farther. Lend thy hand,
    And pluck my magic garment from me. So,

14. amazement frenzy, distraction.

14. piteous full of pity, compassionate.

13–15. * Prospero's short, strong, simple imperatives assert order over the *wild waters* of Miranda's weeping.

15–21. * Shakespeare begins the exposition of the play; with great economy yet emphatic force (e.g. the stressed importance of Miranda in the repeated *thee*) Prospero sketches present and past.

Nouns of relationship occur very frequently in this scene (e.g. father, daughter, mother, brother, uncle, grandmother, sons) one of Prospero's prime purposes being to heal disrupted family bonds.

20–1. * **master ... father** possessor of a very humble cell, and your equally lowly father.

22. meddle mingle (i.e. concern me).

22. 'Tis time the feeling of fulfilment is strong throughout the play, and time is expressed in a variety of ways, in years, days, hours, minutes. After a long and careful preparation, suddenly everything is ready for the successive moments of revelation.

23. * Prospero removes his magician's mantle (decorated perhaps with astrological symbols), having completed the raising and calming of the storm, and only resumes it to speak to Ariel. To Miranda he speaks as father rather than as magus.

25. have comfort let me reassure you.

27. very virtue true essence, very heart of.

28. provision foresight (i.e. he has provided for it).

30. perdition loss

31. Betid happened, befallen.

32. Which whom (i.e. *which thou heard'st* refers to *creature* and *which thou saw'st* to *vessel*).

35. bootless inquisition profitless enquiry (i.e. questions which went unanswered).

36–8. * The attention of the audience, like Miranda's, is arrested and expectation aroused.

36–8. Obey i.e. obey the minute, which *bids* (commands) her to listen.

41. Out fully.

43–4. * **Of ... remembrance** describe any mental picture that has lived in your memory.

43–4. kept with lived, remained, stayed in.

44. 'Tis far off the phrase suggests distance both in time and space; the past is suddenly becoming the present and the remote is being brought near.

45–6. * **And ... warrants** more like a dream than a certainty guaranteed by my memory.

46–7. * Miranda remembers waiting-women rather than her own mother, who seems to have died not long after Miranda was born. (See lines 68–9.)

50. * **dark ... abysm** the deep, dim gulf of the past. The concrete term *abyss* together with *backward* suggests time in terms of space (i.e. Milan is *far off* in time and space).

[Lays down his mantle]

Lie there my art. Wipe thou thine eyes; have comfort.   25
The direful spectacle of the wreck, which touch'd
The very virtue of compassion in thee,
I have with such provision in mine art
So safely ordered that there is no soul –
No, not so much perdition as an hair   30
Betid to any creature in the vessel
Which thou heard'st cry, which thou saw'st sink. Sit
      down,
For thou must now know farther.
Miranda   You have often
Begun to tell me what I am; but stopp'd,
And left me to a bootless inquisition,   35
Concluding 'Stay; not yet'.
Prospero   The hour's now come;
The very minute bids thee ope thine ear.
Obey, and be attentive. Canst thou remember
A time before we came unto this cell?
I do not think thou canst; for then thou wast not   40
Out three years old.
Miranda   Certainly, sir, I can.
Prospero
By what? By any other house, or person?
Of any thing the image, tell me, that
Hath kept with thy remembrance?
Miranda   'Tis far off,
And rather like a dream than an assurance   45
That my remembrance warrants. Had I not
Four, or five, women once, that tended me?
Prospero
Thou hadst, and more, Miranda. But how is it
That this lives in thy mind? What seest thou else
In the dark backward and abysm of time?   50
If thou rememb'rest aught, ere thou cam'st here,
How thou cam'st here thou mayst.

53. * The repeated *twelve year since* emphasizes the length of Prospero's banishment, and also sets Miranda's age at about fifteen, young by modern standards but physically mature enough for marriage.

53. since ago.

55. prince sovereign ruler (rather than 'king's son'). In line 59 Miranda, a Duke's daughter, is described as *princess*.

56. piece of virtue perfect specimen of chastity. (The importance of chastity, purity of conduct before and during marriage, is touched on here by Prospero and stressed by him later in speaking to Ferdinand.)

59. no worse issued of equal birth, blood, nobility.

59–61. * Miranda's words are precisely echoed by Prospero and thus given added emphasis. The idea that good has come out of evil in the past is repeated in Prospero's plan for future reconciliation: he, too, brings good out of evil.

62. heav'd ejected, expelled.

63. holp helped.

64–5. * **To think … remembrance** when I think of the trouble I have made you recall to memory, which I can no longer remember myself.

64–5. farther go on.

66–116. * In these lines Prospero's congested grammatical constructions convey the strong feelings with which he recalls the events leading up to his usurpation. He cannot give a cool and ordered catalogue of incidents but relives the bitter experience as he recounts it.

67. mark me take careful note of what I say. (Perhaps Prospero is hinting that it will be the first and the last time he will tell it.)

68. perfidious treacherous.

70. manage of my state management of my dukedom.

71. signories states (of Northern Italy).

71. the first the principal, most eminent.

72–3. * **Prospero … dignity** Prospero, the principal Duke, holding that rank by virtue of his high reputation.

72–3. liberal arts intellectual studies. (The seven liberal arts were: grammar, logic, rhetoric, arithmetic, geometry, music and astronomy.)

75–7. * **government … studies** the task of governing I put upon my brother's shoulders and neglected my public duties, increasingly carried away and absorbed by my private researches (i.e. into the hidden mysteries of nature and science).

77. false treacherous.

78. * Prospero breaks up his long account of 'the story so far' by repeatedly reproving Miranda for inattention. This is a dramatist's device to provide pauses and rests for actor and audience alike, and could be justified and made to seem natural of Miranda's attention wanders away to the supposed shipwreck.

79–87. * **Being … out on't** once he had mastered the art of saying yes or no to suitors at court, seen whom to promote and whom to restrain for being too pushing, he made those whom I had appointed transfer their loyalty from me to him, changing their allegiance completely. Once he had gained control of

Miranda   But that I do not.
Prospero
  Twelve year since, Miranda, twelve year since,
  Thy father was the Duke of Milan, and
  A prince of power.
Miranda   Sir, are not you my father?   55
Prospero
  Thy mother was a piece of virtue, and
  She said thou wast my daughter; and thy father
  Was Duke of Milan, and his only heir
  And princess no worse issued.
Miranda   O, the heavens!
  What foul play had we that we came from thence?   60
  Or blessed was't we did?
Prospero   Both, both, my girl.
  By foul play, as thou say'st, were we heav'd thence;
  But blessedly holp hither.
Miranda   O, my heart bleeds
  To think o' th' teen that I have turn'd you to,
  Which is from my remembrance. Please you, farther.   65
Prospero
  My brother and thy uncle, call'd Antonio –
  I pray thee, mark me that a brother should
  Be so perfidious. He, whom next thyself
  Of all the world I lov'd, and to him put
  The manage of my state; as at that time   70
  Through all the signories it was the first,
  And Prospero the prime duke, being so reputed
  In dignity, and for the liberal arts
  Without a parallel, those being all my study –
  The government I cast upon my brother   75
  And to my state grew stranger, being transported
  And rapt in secret studies. Thy false uncle –
  Dost thou attend me?
Miranda   Sir, most heedfully.
Prospero
  Being once perfected how to grant suits,

officials and their departments alike, he was able to make everyone in the dukedom dance to whatever tune he chose to play: he had asserted as insidious a stranglehold on the state as ivy does which covers the royal oak, and sapped my authority, draining me of my power in order to increase his.

81. trash for over-topping check a hound which outruns the pack (by attaching a weight or leash to its neck).

83–4. key from the image of a key used in turning a lock, Prospero moves rapidly in his heated imagination to a key in music.

89–93. * I thus ... nature my neglect of matters of state, complete devotion to private study, and the development of my intellect with subjects which, except for being too remote from everyday realities, were worth far more than any ordinary person could appreciate, aroused the evil latent in Antonio's character.

94–6. * The image in *parent* and *beget* continues the references to family bonds. Prospero says that his boundless, unlimited trust in his brother (a proper confidence, like that of any loving parent in trusting its child) produced in Antonio as treacherous a response as Prospero's was trusting.

97–105. * He being ... prerogative Antonio, being placed in a position of lordly power, not only by the income from my estates but also from what my authority could enforce and demand in other ways, like someone who by repeating a lie makes his memory unable to distinguish the true from the false, really believed that he was the Duke, as a result of acting as my deputy and carrying out the public duties of the office with all its privileges.

107–9. * To have ... Milan in order to have no barrier standing between him in his role as deputy and the reality of being Duke, he had to become the Duke of Milan himself, unrestrictedly and unconditionally.

110. temproal royalties duties and functions as a ruler (i.e. wordly rather than spiritual, of State rather than Church).

111. confederates allies himself, joins in league.

How to deny them, who t' advance, and who   80
To trash for over-topping, new created
The creatures that were mine, I say, or chang'd 'em,
Or else new form'd 'em; having both the key
Of officer and office, set all hearts i' th' state
To what tune pleas'd his ear; that now he was   85
The ivy which had hid my princely trunk
And suck'd my verdure out on't. Thou attend'st not.

Miranda

  O, good sir, I do!

Prospero

  I pray thee, mark me.
  I thus neglecting worldly ends, all dedicated
  To closeness and the bettering of my mind   90
  With that which, but by being so retir'd,
  O'er-priz'd all popular rate, in my false brother
  Awak'd an evil nature; and my trust,
  Like a good parent, did beget of him
  A falsehood, in its contrary as great   95
  As my trust was; which had indeed no limit,
  A confidence sans bound. He being thus lorded,
  Not only with that my revenue yielded,
  But what my power might else exact, like one
  Who having into truth, by telling of it,   100
  Made such a sinner of his memory,
  To credit his own lie – he did believe
  He was indeed the Duke; out o' th' substitution,
  And executing th' outward face of royalty
  With all prerogative. Hence his ambition growing –   105
  Dost thou hear?

Miranda   Your tale, sir, would cure deafness.

Prospero

  To have no screen between this part he play'd
  And him he play'd it for, he needs will be
  Absolute Milan. Me, poor man – my library
  Was dukedom large enough – of temporal royalties   110
  He thinks me now incapable; confederates,

112. * So dry ... sway so thirsty was he for power.

114. * Subject ... crown i.e. makes Antonio's ducal coronet owe allegiance to Alonso's royal crown.

114–15. * bend ... unbow'd make Milan kneel (never having kow-towed to any state before) submissively (to Naples).

117. * Mark ... th'event note carefully the contract (made with Alonso) and what the outcome was.

118–20. * I should ... sons Miranda suggests that she would be breaking one of the Commandments (i.e. not honouring her father's mother) if she had anything less than the highest regard for her. Rather than think that Antonio was only a bastard-brother to her father, Miranda prefers to accept the fact that even the best families can produce 'black sheep' occasionally.

123–6. * in lieu ... dukedom according to the conditions agreed upon (the receiving of both homage and a great sum of tribute money) would in return at once evict me and my family from the dukedom.

127–32. * Whereon ... crying self the economy of these lines shows Shakespeare at his most masterly: we can see the army which has been specially raised by Alonso waiting to crush any loyal opposition; hear twelve striking from the city clocks; watch Antonio, perhaps there in person, drawing back the bolts of the great gates of Milan; and listen in the silence of the dead of night to the crying of the little child as the specially appointed agents, like evil spirits of midnight, hurry Prospero and his daughter away.

134–5. * a hint ... to't an occasion which forces tears from my eyes.

136. business matter, affair. The word is often used in the sense of intrigue or plot (e.g. line 142).

138. impertinent irrelevant.
139. wench lass (a term of affection, not only for a servant).

140. provokes prompts, raises.
140. durst dared.

So dry he was for sway, wi' th' King of Naples,
To give him annual tribute, do him homage,
Subject his coronet to his crown, and bend
The dukedom, yet unbow'd – alas, poor Milan! –   115
To most ignoble stooping.
Miranda   O the heavens!
Prospero
  Mark his condition, and th' event, then tell me
  If this might be a brother.
Miranda   I should sin
  'To think but nobly of my grandmother:
  Good wombs have borne bad sons.
Prospero   Now the condition: 120
  This King of Naples, being an enemy
  To me inveterate, hearkens my brother's suit;
  Which was, that he, in lieu o' th' premises,
  Of homage, and I know not how much tribute,
  Should presently extirpate me and mine   125
  Out of the dukedom, and confer fair Milan
  With all the honours on my brother. Whereon,
  A treacherous army levied, one midnight
  Fated to th' purpose, did Antonio open
  The gates of Milan; and, i' th' dead of darkness,   130
  The ministers for th' purpose hurried thence
  Me and thy crying self.
Miranda   Alack, for pity!
  I, not rememb'ring how I cried out then,
  Will cry it o'er again; it is a hint
  That wrings mine eyes to't.
Prospero   Hear a little further,   135
  And then I'll bring thee to the present business
  Which now's upon 's; without the which this story
  Were most impertinent.
Miranda   Wherefore did they not
  That hour destroy us?
Prospero   Well demanded, wench!
  My tale provokes that question. Dear, they durst not,   140

141–2. * nor set ... bloody i.e. unlike staghunters who openly blooded themselves at the kill.

143. * With ... ends with more pleasant colours (than blood-red) disguised their intentions. (To 'paint' usually meant to cover up by using cosmetics.)

144. In few briefly, in a few words.

144. bark ship (barque).

146. carcass of a butt skeleton of a tub, a small, leaky boat, little more than wooden ribs, a mere decomposing corpse of a dinghy. (It has been suggested that Shakespeare wrote 'buss', a Flemish fishing vessel.)

147. tackle ropes.

148. hoist placed (lit. lifted).

149–51. * To cry ... wrong the compressed vividness of the whole of this speech excites the imagination, and nowhere is it more satisfying than here, with the rhyme *cry ... sigh*, the fluctuating movement of the words, and the idea that the natural world of wind and sea sympathises with the innocent victims of an unnatural act.

149. roar'd though commonly used of lions and cannon, the word often meant 'loud lamentation': when Prospero and Miranda *cry to th'sea* in weeping, the sea answers by lamenting, and when they subside to exhausted sighing, the winds respond with similar expressions of sympathy.

151. loving wrong i.e. though sympathetic, the winds might have done them wrong by upsetting their little craft. (The phrase is an example of the figure of speech known as oxymoron.)

152. cherubin little angel.

154. Infused inspired.

155. drops full salt Prospero's bitter, stinging tears are as salt as the sea he is weeping into. Abandoned by man, he finds a relationship with nature, though consolation only comes from Miranda.

155. deck'd covered, adorned.

156. burden (a) load (of grief), (b) bass or undersong (compare line 380), (c) birth-pangs. All three meanings are present in some degree: Prospero is 'in travail' in his grief, groaning out a melancholy music, and weighed down by his sorrow. Only out of the pain of this delivery will a happy future life, a rebirth, eventually come.

156–8. * which ... ensue your smile produced a spirit of endurance in me, and encouraged me to endure whatever might follow.

161. * Gonzalo's name is now given to the audience as well as to Miranda.

162. charity kindness, love (the Christian loving-kindness of St. Paul's Faith, Hope and Charity in *I Corinthians* XIII).

162–3. * appointed ... design put in charge of this plot.

164. Rich garments perhaps so that Prospero could maintain some dignity should he reach an inhabited shore. They are used in Act IV to distract the conspirators from murdering him, and in Act V to enable him to 'rise from the dead' and present himself as the rightful Duke.

164. stuffs materials, cloths.

165. steaded stood me in good stead, been very useful.

165. gentleness noble nature, behaviour of a Christian gentleman.

So dear the love my people bore me; nor set
A mark so bloody on the business; but
With colours fairer painted their foul ends.
In few, they hurried us aboard a bark;
Bore us some leagues to sea, where they prepared   145
A rotten carcass of a butt, not rigg'd,
Nor tackle, sail, nor mast; the very rats
Instinctively have quit it. There they hoist us,
To cry to th' sea, that roar'd to us; to sigh
To th' winds, whose pity, sighing back again,   150
Did us but loving wrong.
Miranda   Alack, what trouble
Was I then to you!
Prospero   O, a cherubin
Thou wast that did preserve me! Thou didst smile,
Infused with a fortitude from heaven,
When I have deck'd the sea with drops full salt,   155
Under my burden groan'd; which rais'd in me
An undergoing stomach, to bear up
Against what should ensue.
Miranda   How came we ashore?
Prospero
By Providence divine.
Some food we had and some fresh water that   160
A noble Neapolitan, Gonzalo,
Out of his charity, who being then appointed
Master of this design, did give us, with
Rich garments, linens, stuffs, and necessaries,
Which since have steaded much; so, of his gentleness,   165

166. furnish;d provided, equipped.

167. volumes Prospero's books containing magic lore (which Caliban understands the value of: see Act III, Scene ii, lines 85, 88 and 91).

168. above more highly than.

169. Now I arise i.e. to put on his magician's robe and charm Miranda asleep so that he can speak to his spirit-servant, Ariel. 'Arise' may also refer to his rising fortunes (see lines 178–9).

170. Sit still remain seated, stay sitting. (From this position she will more easily be able to relax into a sleeping one.)

170. the last the conclusion.

171–4. * and here … careful Prospero has been a better teacher than most princesses are lucky enough to get, and has taught her more than most princesses learn, who have more opportunities for distraction and less conscientious tutors. (The education of princes, i.e. rulers, was of great concern in the 16th and 17th centuries, and Shakespeare may be making a point of particular interest to the learned James I.)

176. 'tis beating (a) the question why Prospero raised the storm, (b) the sea-sound of the storm itself.

177. thus far forth this much, as far as this.

178–84. * By accident … droop by an amazing chance, generous Mistress Fortune, now at last graciously smiling on me, has brought my enemies to our very shores; and by my foreknowledge I have discovered that reaching the summit of my fortunes depends upon a highly favourable star, whose astrological influence I must now woo, for if I fail to take this opportunity my fortunes will decline for ever from this moment.

178–84. influence the power over men's destinites which 'flowed in' from the planets and stars, according to ancient and medieval astrology.

185. dullness sleepiness.

186. give it way allow it to come (i.e. don't try to fight it).

187. Come away servant 'come here, my servant'. Prospero makes it clear that he is Ariel's master before addressing him by name.

Stage Direction. **Enter Ariel** In costume probably of sky-blue, in movement graceful and lively, Ariel, played by a boy with an unbroken voice, personifies the speed of thought and the freedom of the imagination.

Knowing I lov'd my books, he furnish'd me
From mine own library with volumes that
I prize above my dukedom.
Miranda   Would I might
But ever see that man!
Prospero   Now I arise.

[Puts on his mantle]

Sit still, and hear the last of our sea-sorrow.   170
Here in this island we arriv'd; and here
Have I, thy schoolmaster, made thee more profit
Than other princess' can, that have more time
For vainer hours, and tutors not so careful.
Miranda
Heavens thank you for't! And now, I pray you, sir,   175
For still 'tis beating in my mind, your reason
For raising this sea-storm?
Prospero   Know thus far forth:
By accident most strange, bountiful Fortune,
Now my dear lady, hath mine enemies
Brought to this shore; and by my prescience   180
I find my zenith doth depend upon
A most auspicious star, whose influence
If now I court not, but omit, my fortunes
Will ever after droop. Here cease more questions;
Thou art inclin'd to sleep; 'tis a good dullness,   185
And give it way. I know thou canst not choose.

[MIRANDA sleeps]

Come away, servant; come; I am ready now.
Approach, my Ariel. Come.

189. * In his ceremonious greeting, with its open-vowelled assonance, *hail ... great ... grave ... hail,* Ariel acknowledges his master as a good white-magician.

190–2. * **answer ... pleasure** 'obey your wishes fully and exactly'. Ariel is Prospero's agent: his highly active role is suggested not only by his physical movements, but by his language, which is full of verbs. In these lines his spir-itual nature is seen in his ability to enter all four elements, swimming in water, diving into fire, riding on air, and (line 255) doing business in the earth.

192–3. * **To ... quality** employ Ariel and all his fellow-spirits at your power-ful command.

194. Perform'd to point exactly (in every detail) managed.

195. To every article to the letter, in every respect.

196–7. beak pointed prow.

196–7. waist amidships.

196–7. deck poop-deck. (Ariel has gone from bow to stern, horizontally, before moving vertically, ascending from the rigging.)

198. flam'd amazement 'filling everyone with fear and wonder at my fiery appearance'. Ariel is in the element of fire, St Elmo's Fire, caused by static electricity, and mentioned in travel books of the period.

200. yards yard-arms, on which the sails hang.

200. distinctly in several places at once.

201–6. * Ariel is enjoying re-living his experiences and the exercise of Puck-ish power.

201. precursors forerunners, harbingers (going ahead to announce the approach of a king, i.e. Jupiter, the king of Heaven, and his thunder).

203–4. fire and cracks lightning and thunder, like the flash and explosion of cannon.

203–4. sulphurous roaring lightning and thunder.

203–4. Neptune god of the ocean.

205. * Compare lines 3–5 and see note. Neptune's *bold waves* (valiant troops) *tremble* (shake with fear) at Jove's siege-weapons.

206. dread trident Neptune's dreaded three-pronged spear, symbol of his power and majesty, shakes with fear (as the sea is shaken by the onslaught from the sky).

207. coil tumult, turmoil, uproar.

208. infect affect, disturb.

208–10. * **Not ... desperation** there was not a person on board who did not feel the frenzy which madmen feel, or did not perform strange, even suicidal actions.

212. Ferdinand the audience is now given his name.

213. up-staring standing on end (with fear).

213. like reeds i.e. stiff with terror. (Compare the desscription of Gonzalo's beard in Act V, Scene i, line 17 as *eaves of reeds,* or thatch).

214. Hell is empty i.e. all the devils have left Hell to plague the ship.

[Enter ARIEL]

Ariel
    All hail, great master! grave sir, hail! I come
    To answer thy best pleasure; be't to fly,   190
    To swim, to dive into the fire, to ride
    On the curl'd clouds. To thy strong bidding task
    Ariel and all his quality.
Prospero   Hast thou, spirit,
    Perform'd to point the tempest that I bade thee?
Ariel
    To every article.   195
    I boarded the King's ship; now on the beak,
    Now in the waist, the deck, in every cabin,
    I flam'd amazement. Sometime I'd divide,
    And burn in many places; on the topmast,
    The yards, and bowsprit, would I flame distinctly,   200
    Then meet and join. Jove's lightning, the precursors
    O' th' dreadful thunder-claps, more momentary
    And sight-outrunning were not; the fire and cracks
    Of sulphurous roaring the most mighty Neptune
    Seem to besiege, and make his bold waves tremble,   205
    Yea, his dread trident shake.
Prospero   My brave spirit!
    Who was so firm, so constant, that this coil
    Would not infect his reason?
Ariel   Not a soul
    But felt a fever of the mad, and play'd
    Some tricks of desperation. All but mariners   210
    Plung'd in the foaming brine, and quit the vessel,
    Then all afire with me; the King's son, Ferdinand,
    With hair up-staring – then like reeds, not hair –
    Was the first man that leapt; cried 'Hell is empty,
    And all the devils are here.'
Prospero   Why, that's my spirit!   215
    But was not this nigh shore?
Ariel   Close by, my master.

217. * No ... perish'd as Prospero has already told Miranda in line 30. He assumed that his order to preserve Alonso's courtiers intact and unblemished had been obeyed by Ariel, and Ariel is here reporting his mission successfully completed.

218. sustaining garments clothes which gave them buoyancy, kept them afloat.

220. troops groups.

222. cooling of the air this suggests a hot day on which Ferdinand is cooling the air around him with his breath (compare blowing on hot porridge), but also a picture of him cooling down after the fiery excitement of leaving the ship (and now sorrowfully 'cooling his heels' alone).

223. odd angle out-of-the-way corner.

224. sad knot to have folded arms (*knot*) was a sign of melancholy. Ferdinand believes he is the sole survivor of the wreck and is mourning his father's loss in particular. Ariel mischievously imitates *this*, his posture.

226. in harbour in an anchorage, sheltered.

227. deep nook creek or inlet (deep enough in water to float a sea-going vessel, and perhaps also a deep enough cleft to hide it, masts and hull, from discovery by land).

228. * midnight ... dew dew for magical charms had to be gathered at midnight (the witching hour); the foul witch Sycorax also uses dew (for evil purposes), see line 321.

229. still-vex'd Bermoothes the Bermudas, constantly troubled by winds and storms. Shakespeare places Prospero's island, without any geographical precision, somewhere in the Mediterranean between Naples and Tunis; this reference to the West Indies (reminding us of the *Sea-Adventure* episode in 1609) is perhaps chiefly included to show Ariel's powers of flight, and his ability to cover in a short time a distance which would have taken a sailing vessel weeks of dangerous voyaging to accomplish.

231. * charm ... labour a spell added to the toil they have undergone.

234. flote sea, ocean-wave.

237. great person Alonso's royal self.

239. mid-season noon.

240. two glasses two hours (measured by the hour-glass), i.e. it is now 2 p.m. The repeated references to time give the play its sense of urgency and inevitability.

241. * spent ... preciously i.e. they cannot afford to waste valuable time. (Time is precious because it is in short supply.)

242–6. * Magician's could control spirits only by continual effort, and Ariel's rebelliousness would be understood by Shakespeare's audience. Shakespeare uses the quarrel (which is only resolved at line 296) principally to introduce his next character, Caliban, before he appears.

242. pains work, labour.

243. remember remind.

Prospero
  But are they, Ariel, safe?
Ariel   Not a hair perish'd;
  On their sustaining garments not a blemish,
  But fresher than before; and, as thou bad'st me,
  In troops I have dispers'd them 'bout the isle.   220
  The King's son have I landed by himself,
  Whom I left cooling of the air with sighs
  In an odd angle of the isle, and sitting,
  His arms in this sad knot.
Prospero   Of the King's ship,
  The mariners, say how thou hast dispos'd,   225
  And all the rest o' th' fleet?
Ariel   Safely in harbour
  Is the King's ship; in the deep nook, where once
  Thou call'dst me up at midnight to fetch dew
  From the still-vex'd Bermoothes, there she's hid;
  The mariners all under hatches stowed,   230
  Who, with a charm join'd to their suffer'd labour,
  I have left asleep; and for the rest o' th' fleet,
  Which I dispers'd, they all have met again,
  And are upon the Mediterranean flote
  Bound sadly home for Naples,   235
  Supposing that they saw the King's ship wreck'd,
  And his great person perish.
Prospero   Ariel, thy charge
  Exactly is perform'd; but there's more work.
  What is the time o' th' day?
Ariel   Past the mid season.
Prospero
  At least two glasses. The time 'twixt six and now   240
  Must by us both be spent most preciously.
Ariel
  Is there more toil? Since thou dost give me pains,
  Let me remember thee what thou hast promis'd,
  Which is not yet perform'd me.

244. moody 'bolshie', discontented.

246. out finished (i.e. time is up).

249. grudge complaining, murmuring (compare line 294).

250. bate me 'reduce my length of service by'.

252–6. * Ariel's capacity to move through every element is again referred to.
252–3. * **ooze ... deep** ocean bed.

255–6. * **veins ... frost** in the subterranean streams which flow like veins through the earth's 'body' even when the surface is hardened by frost.

257. malignant rebellious.
258. Sycorax a name (found only in *The Tempest*) formed perhaps from a combination of the Greek *sys* (sow) and *korax* (raven) but also possibly deriving from *Coraxi*, the tribe from which the enchantress Circe came. (Circe was the sorceress in Homer's *Odyssey* who turned men into swine.)

261. Argier Algiers.
261. O was she so? Prospero's reply seems to be sarcastic, as if Ariel were mistaken, but he does not supply any alternative.
263. damn'd i.e. to hell. Sycorax and her *sorceries terrible* contrast with Prospero's beneficent magic. She was banished from Algiers for *mischiefs manifold* (countless crimes), Prospero from Milan for the bettering of his mind (line 90). Further parallels and contrasts are that both are brought, in slightly different senses, to the island 'with child'; both are able to employ Ariel as a servant; both spend twelve years on the island. It is as if Shakespeare by means of these similarities is stressing the contrast between Prospero's white magic and Sycorax's black magic.
266–7. * **one thing ... life** this is unexplained, but may be that she was pregnant (line 269, *with child*).

Prospero   How now, moody?
   What is 't thou canst demand?
Ariel   My liberty.   245
Prospero
   Before the time be out? No more!
Ariel   I prithee,
   Remember I have done thee worthy service,
   Told thee no lies, made thee no mistakings, serv'd
   Without or grudge or grumblings. Thou didst
      promise
   To bate me a full year.
Prospero   Dost thou forget   250
   From what a torment I did free thee?
Ariel   No.
Prospero
   Thou dost; and think'st it much to tread the ooze
   Of the salt deep,
   To run upon the sharp wind of the north,
   To do me business in the veins o' th' earth   255
   When it is bak'd with frost.
Ariel   I do not, sir.
Prospero
   Thou liest, malignant thing. Hast thou forgot
   The foul witch Sycorax, who with age and envy
   Was grown into a hoop? Hast thou forgot her?
Ariel
   No, sir.
Prospero
   Thou hast. Where was she born? Speak, tell me.   260
Ariel
   Sir, in Argier.
Prospero   O, was she so? I must
   Once in a month recount what thou hast been,
   Which thou forget'st. This damn'd witch Sycorax,
   For mischiefs manifold, and sorceries terrible
   To enter human hearing, from Argier   265
   Thou know'st was banish'd; for one thing she did
   They would not take her life. Is not this true?

269. blue-eyed blue-lidded eyes, an indication of pregnancy.

272–3. * spirit … commands because Ariel is a spirit of air he cannot carry out orders which are repellant to him since they come from a witch who works by means of the lowest element, earth. Her son, Caliban, is addressed as *thou earth* (line 314).

274. grand hests powerful commands.

275. potent ministers powerful spirits (of evil).

276. unmitigable implacable.

280. vent utter.

281. strike strike the water as they revolve.

281–4. * Then … shape Sycorax gave birth in animal fashion (*did litter*) to a monster (an abortion, a misshapen creature).

281–4. freckled spotted (perhaps like a venomous toad or snake). The handsome Ferdinand, a direct contrast physically and morally to Caliban, is *honour'd with a human shape* (he *carries a brave form*, line 412), and in the Masque scene (Act IV, Scene i, line 105) Juno goes to bless the union of Ferdinand and Miranda, that they may be *honour'd in their issue*.

284. Caliban the name is possibly a rough anagram of cannibal.

285. Dull slow-witted (in fact, just what Ariel is *not*).

287. groans the groans of Ariel as prisoner contrast with his songs when free.

288. * wolves … bears perhaps incongruous on a Mediterranean island or in the Bahamas, but Prospero's island is imaginary rather then real. So moving were Ariel's agonized groans that even the most ferocious beasts felt sympathy.

289–90. * torment … damn'd a torture to impose in those condemned to Hell (a punishment, e.g. solitary confinement, meted out to the convicted).

291. again undo i.e. the decision having been made could not be reversed, was irrevocable (compare *What's done cannot be undone* in *Macbeth*: i.e. the dead cannot be brought to life again). Prospero's power is greater than Sycorax's not only in being able to release Ariel physically, but to undo the locked situation of the past, and by foregiveness to release those held prisoner by their guilt.

294. rend an oak (compare Act V, Scene i, line 45). To rend an oak would be to show greater strength than to rift a pine, and an oak would be a stronger prison than a pine.

296. twelve winters i.e. your previous sentence will be repeated (only in the even more restricting inner recesses of an oak this time).

Ariel
  Ay, sir.
Prospero
  This blue-ey'd hag was hither brought with child,
  And here was left by th' sailors. Thou, my slave,   270
  As thou report'st thyself, wast then her servant;
  And, for thou wast a spirit too delicate
  To act her earthy and abhorr'd commands,
  Refusing her grand hests, she did confine thee,
  By help of her more potent ministers,   275
  And in her most unmitigable rage,
  Into a cloven pine; within which rift
  Imprison'd thou didst painfully remain
  A dozen years; within which space she died,
  And left thee there, where thou didst vent thy groans
  As fast as mill-wheels strike. Then was this island –
  Save for the son that she did litter here,   280
  A freckl'd whelp, hag-born – not honour'd with
  A human shape.
Ariel   Yes, Caliban her son.
Prospero
  Dull thing, I say so; he, that Caliban   285
  Whom now I keep in service. Thou best know'st
  What torment I did find thee in; thy groans
  Did make wolves howl, and penetrate the breasts
  Of ever-angry bears; it was a torment
  To lay upon the damn'd, which Sycorax   290
  Could not again undo. It was mine art,
  When I arriv'd and heard thee, that made gape
  The pine, and let thee out.
Ariel   I thank thee, master.
Prospero
  If thou more murmur'st, I will rend an oak
  And peg thee in his knotty entrails, till   295
  Thou hast howl'd away twelve winters.

297–8. * **I will … gently** I will obey your orders and perform my tasks as a spirit graciously (i.e. ungrudgingly, as a 'gentleman', with cheerful humility).

301. nymph o' th' sea e.g. from a blue costume to a green one. Ariel is still, as at all times, invisible to everyone but Prospero, and his new appearance is both to delight the audience with a fresh vision of spectacular beauty and to remind them of the sea (particularly as he sings his sea songs to Ferdinand). His frequent changes of costume also echo the central theme of transformation in the play.

303. shape appearance, disguise.

304. diligence speed, despatch.

307. Heaviness drowsiness, sleepiness.

309. villain churl, low servant.

311. miss him do without him.

312. serves in offices performs duties.

314. * Caliban's den perhaps stands close to Prospero's cell, at the rear of the stage, like a dog-kennel (*here you sty me*, line 342). The audience's expectation is aroused by hearing Caliban's earthy voice, full of *grudge or grumblings* (line 249), before seeing him.

314. thou earth you clod.

316. tortoise i.e. slow-witted and cumbersome.

Stage Direction. **Re-enter Ariel** Ariel's change of costume was a simple one, taking only ten lines to complete. Both his appearance (*Fine apparition*) and his prompt willingness are in striking contrast to Caliban.

317. quaint handsome, elegant.

318. * The whispered instruction (to fetch Ferdinand) arouses our curiosity and continues to show Prospero 'stage-managing' the events.

Ariel   Pardon, master;
  I will be correspondent to command,
  And do my spriting gently.
Prospero   Do so; and after two days
  I will discharge thee.
Ariel   That's my noble master!
  What shall I do? Say what. What shall I do?   300
Prospero
  Go make thyself like a nymph o' th' sea; be subject
  To no sight but thine and mine, invisible
  To every eyeball else. Go take this shape,
  And hither come in 't. Go, hence with diligence!

                [Exit ARIEL]

  Awake, dear heart, awake; thou hast slept well;   305
  Awake.
Miranda The strangeness of your story put
  Heaviness in me.
Prospero   Shake it off. Come on,
  We'll visit Caliban, my slave, who never
  Yields us kind answer.
Miranda   'Tis a villain, sir,
  I do not love to look on.
Prospero   But as 'tis,   310
  We cannot miss him: he does make our fire,
  Fetch in our wood, and serves in offices
  That profit us. What ho! slave! Caliban!
  Thou earth, thou! Speak.
Caliban [Within] There's wood enough within.
Prospero
  Come forth, I say; there's other business for thee.   315
  Come, thou tortoise! when?

          [Re-enter ARIEL like a water-nymph]

  Fine apparition! My quaint Ariel,
  Hark in thine ear.

319–20. * got ... dam the Devil himself has possessed Sycorax and sired Caliban.

321–4. * As wicked ... all o'er the poisonous dew collected by Sycorax contrasts with that collected by Ariel (line 228) and is appropriately gathered with a raven's feather (see note to line **258**). The south-west wind was thought to bring fever, and some Elizabethan houses were built so that no windows faced south.

326. * pen ... up make you gasp for breath.

326. pen restrict.

326. urchins goblins in the shape of hedgehogs.

327–8. * Shall ... thee shall issue forth during that empty waste period of darkness (when they do their work as spirits of darkness) so that they can torment (*work All exercise on*) you.

328–30. * thou ... made 'em Caliban will be nipped or stung so thick and fast that he will become riddled, a veritable honeycomb, every sting being more painful than any given by bees which make the cells of a honeycomb.

328–30. pinch used several times in the play both for physical affliction and for mental anguish, suggests tortures in which pincers were used.

330. * I must ... dinner Caliban, cowed for a moment, changes the subject and consoles himself with the thought of food. He is shown immediately as a creature of appetite, with his mind, such as it is, on physical satisfactions.

331–2. * This ... from me Prospero appears to have taken the island from Caliban, but 17th century thought considered that Prospero had a natural right to rule the inferior *deformed slave*: perhaps he made a mistake in trying to educate Caliban beyond his capacity to be civilized.

333. strok'st me i.e. like a pet.

334. berries perhaps cedar-berries (used in water by the castaways in Jourdain's *A Discovery of the Bermudas,* 1610).

334–6. * teach ... night by using the words *the bigger light* and *the less*, rather than 'the sun' and 'the moon', Shakespeare gives us a glimpse of Caliban's actual lessons as he develops a vocabulary and also suggests a primitive awe, a sun and moon worship. (The phrase probably comes from *Genesis*, Chapter I, Verse 16 and may suggest that at first the island was an Eden of innocence.)

337. qualities natural properties, i.e. what the island had to offer.

338. * In a single line of finely-patterned alliteration, Shakespeare conjures up a picture of the island, parts of which are life-giving (*springs* and *fertile*) and parts sterile (*brine-pits* and *barren place*).

339. charms spells.

340. light alight, descend.

340. toads etc.: associated with witches.

342. sty me coop me up (as in a pigsty).

Ariel
> My lord, it shall be done.

> [Exit]

Prospero
> Thou poisonous slave, got by the devil himself
> Upon thy wicked dam, come forth! 320

> [Enter CALIBAN]

Caliban
> As wicked dew as e'er my mother brush'd
> With raven's feather from unwholesome fen
> Drop on you both! A south-west blow on ye
> And blister you all o'er!

Prospero
> For this, be sure, to-night thou shalt have cramps, 325
> Side-stitches that shall pen thy breath up; urchins
> Shall, for that vast of night that they may work,
> All exercise on thee; thou shalt be pinch'd
> As thick as honeycomb, each pinch more stinging
> Than bees that made 'em.

Caliban   I must eat my dinner. 330
> This island's mine, by Sycorax my mother,
> Which thou tak'st from me. When thou cam'st first,
> Thou strok'st me and made much of me, wouldst
>   give me
> Water with berries in't, and teach me how
> To name the bigger light, and how the less, 335
> That burn by day and night; and then I lov'd thee,
> And show'd thee all the qualities o' th' isle,
> The fresh springs, brine-pits, barren place and fertile.
> Curs'd be I that did so! All the charms
> Of Sycorax, toads, beetles, bats, light on you! 340
> For I am all the subjects that you have,
> Which first was mine own king; and here you sty me
> In this hard rock, whiles you do keep from me
> The rest o' th' island.

345. stripes lashes, flogging.

345. move stir, make respond.

345. us'd treated.

346. human humane (*with humane care:* kindly, humanely).

347–8. * Caliban's attempted rape of Miranda contrasts strongly with the restrained behaviour of Ferdinand (see Act IV, Scene i, lines 23–31).

351. Abhorred revolting, disgusting.

352. * **any print ... all ill** the image is from printing. Miranda cannot imprint or impress on Caliban's unreceptive nature any idea of honourable behaviour because he is susceptible only to evil.

355–8. * **When ... known** when you were unable, in your primitive state, to put your thoughts into words, and could only express yourself in animal sounds, I gave you the gift of language so that you could communicate what you were thinking.

358. thy vile race your low nature. (*vile* is 'low-born' and *race* is 'inherited nature'.)

359. good noble (in antithesis to *vile*).

352–62. * Some editors give this speech to Prospero because the severity of Miranda's words may seem out of character. Her horror of Caliban, particularly since she has shown a trusting kindness towards him, expresses a natural revulsion which is perfectly understandable, however.

363. profit on't the best thing I have derived from it.

364. red plague the other two plague sores were the yellow and the black.

364. rid kill, destroy.

365. learning teaching.

365. Hag-seed child of a witch. Prospero vigorously answers Caliban's alliterative abuse (*red ... rid, learning ... language*) with his own (*Hag-seed ... hence, Fetch ... fuel*).

366. * **And ... business** and you would be well advised to perform any other tasks promptly.

367. Shrug'st thou Caliban has made a gesture of indifference and defiance.

367. malice malicious brute (i.e. creature with the power to harm, not merely spitefully-minded: see Act III, Scene ii, lines 83–7).

368. thou neglect'st you are negligent.

369. rack torture (put on the rack).

369. old of old people (e.g. arthritic pains).

370. bones with aches perhaps a hint of the consequences of venereal disease (sometimes known as the 'Neopolitan bone-ache') which would be a suitable punishment for Caliban's lack of sexual restraint. (if Caliban is thought of as an innocent, natural and primitive savage of the New World, then Prospero's threats of European tortures and diseases can be interpreted as the less pleasant contributions made by the Old World to the New.)

370. aches ws pronounced 'aitches'.

371. beasts tremble compare the effects of Ariel's groans.

373. Setebos 'the great devil Setebos' of the Patagonians (mentioned in Eden's *History of Travel*, 1577).

Prospero   Thou most lying slave,
  Whom stripes may move, not kindness! I have us'd
       thee,   345
  Filth as thou art, with human care, and lodg'd thee
  In mine own cell, till thou didst seek to violate
  The honour of my child.
Caliban
  O ho, O ho! Would't had been done.   350
  Thou didst prevent me; I had peopl'd else
  This isle with Calibans.
Miranda   Abhorred slave,
  Which any print of goodness wilt not take,
  Being capable of all ill! I pitied thee,
  Took pains to make thee speak, taught thee each
       hour   355
  One thing or other. When thou didst not, savage,
  Know thine own meaning, but wouldst gabble like
  A thing most brutish, I endow'd thy purposes
  With words that made them known. But thy vile race,
  Though thou didst learn, had that in't which good
       natures   360
  Could not abide to be with; therefore wast thou
  Deservedly confin'd into this rock, who hadst
  Deserv'd more than a prison.
Caliban
  You taught me language, and my profit on't
  Is, I know how to curse. The red plague rid you
  For learning me your language!
Prospero   Hag-seed, hence!   365
  Fetch us in fuel. And be quick, thou 'rt best,
  To answer other business. Shrug'st thou, malice?
  If thou neglect'st, or dost unwillingly
  What I command, I'll rack thee with old cramps,
  Fill all thy bones with aches, make thee roar,   370
  That beasts shall tremble at thy din.
Caliban   No, pray thee.
  [Aside] I must obey. His art is of such pow'r,
  It would control my dam's god, Setebos,

374. vassal slave.

Stage Direction. **Exit Caliban** Caliban's departure, immediately followed by the arrival of Ferdinand, presents an almost literally 'black and white' contrast.

Stage Direction. **Re-enter Ariel** Ariel accompanies his singing, probably on a lute. The irresistibly attractive power of music is seen for the first time in the play, and occurs again at frequent intervals; by means of it, Ariel moves the actors at 'stage-manager' Prospero's bidding.

375–80. * Ariel's song bids his fellow spirits to:

(a) come to the golden beaches of the island (375) as if to a great hall in which they will dance,

(b) *take hands* (376) to begin their ceremonious dance, and when they have

(c) *curtsied* (377), i.e. 'done courtesy' by bowing to each other and kissed the waves, which are still turbulent from the tempest, into silence (*whist*) in lines 377–8, (alternatively, 'having kissed each other now that the waves have been hushed') then to

(d) dance, *foot it*, gracefully, *featly*, (379) and also

(e) accompany his song by singing a refrain, *burden* to it (380).

381–6. * The origins and purpose of these lines are obscure. The *bow-wow* may refer to sounds made at ceremonial Virginian dances of the time, and perhaps the *watch-dogs* and *strutting chanticleer* suggest the arrival of dawn when those spirits who were released at midnight to visit the world were required to return to the underworld.

387. * **Where … earth?** the *burden* has been sung *dispersedly*, i.e. from various parts of the stage, above it in the upper stage and perhaps under it.

389. waits upon attends. A god or goddess would be attended by the divine power of music. Miranda is taken for a goddess (line 422) by Ferdinand, and Prospero is virtually *god o' th' island*.

391. again again and again, repeatedly.

391. wreck shipwrecking.

392. crept by me stole past me (i.e. moved slowly and stealthily, tiptoed).

393. Allaying soothing. Miranda uses *allay* in the second line of her first speech, and like Ferdinand's her weeping is calmed by Prospero as he calms the tempest. Before they even meet, the lovers are united by using similar words and actions.

393. Passion sorrow, passionate grief.

394. air tune.

397–405. * Ariel's song to Ferdinand

(a) confirms his fears that his father is dead, by telling him that he is lying in thirty feet of water, and (b) tries to reconcile him to the fact by saying that he (the King) is undergoing a physical transformation which will be different from the usual processes of decay: this *sea-change* will make him a precious object (of *coral* and *pearl*) rather than mere 'dust'. Alonso's transformation into *something rich and strange* is to be a spiritual one rather than of that part of him *that doth fade,* his body.

And make a vassal of him.
Prospero   So, slave; hence!

[Exit CALIBAN]

[Re-enter ARIEL invisible, playing and singing;
FERDINAND following]

[ARIEL'S Song]

> Come unto these yellow sands,   375
>   And then take hands;
> Curtsied when you have and kiss'd,
>   The wild waves whist,
> Foot it featly here and there,
> And, sweet sprites, the burden bear.   380
>   Hark, hark!
> [Burden dispersedly] Bow-wow.
>   The watch dogs bark.
> [Burden dispersedly] Bow-wow.
>   Hark, hark! I hear   385
> The strain of strutting chanticleer
>   Cry, Cock-a-diddle-dow.

Ferdinand
Where should this music be? I' th' air or th' earth?
It sounds no more; and sure it waits upon
Some god o' th' island. Sitting on a bank,   390
Weeping again the King my father's wreck,
This music crept by me upon the waters,
Allaying both their fury and my passion
With its sweet air; thence I have follow'd it,
Or it hath drawn me rather. But 'tis gone.   395
No, it begins again.

[ARIEL'S Song]

> Full fathom five thy father lies;
>   Of his bones are coral made;
> Those are pearls that were his eyes;
>   Nothing of him that doth fade   400

403. hourly ring his knell toll his passing-bell (tolled at his funeral) every hour, as befits the passing away of a king.

404. * This dirge-like *burden* contrasts with the rousing animation of the watchdogs and cock.

406. * **The ditty ... father** the words of this song commemorate my father's death by drowning.

407–8. mortal business (this singing is no) human affair.

407–8. owes owns, possesses.

409–10. * **The fringed ... yond** Prospero tells Miranda to raise (*advance*) her eyes (*fringed curtains* are literally her eyelids with their eyelashes) and tell him what she sees over there (*yond*). If Prospero and Miranda have withdrawn to the inner stage before Ferdinand's arrival, then the metaphor of curtained eyes may derive from a curtained inner stage.

412. brave form noble appearance. Perhaps there is a note of disappointment in *But 'tis a spirit*.

415–16. * Prospero uses (a) the image of staining: Ferdinand's salt tears have affected his appearance (whereas the salt sea has not stained his or the courtiers' garments), and (b) the image of a worm (*canker*) eating into a beautiful bud or petal (i.e. his cheek).

417. fellows companions, associates.

419. natural belonging to nature (i.e. not spiritual).

420–21. * **It ... prompts its** Ferdinand and Miranda are free agents and Prospero can only 'prompt' them by arranging that they meet. He is delighted to see that his plan is working. (*It goes on.*)

422. goddess the lovers' responses to each other continue to be identical. To him, she is a *goddess*; to her, he is a *thing divine*.

423. airs musical sounds, melodies, songs (compare line 394).

423–4. * **Vouchsafe ... know** grant my request to know.

423–4. remain dwell.

425. good instruction helpful information.

426. bear me conduct myself, behave.

426–8. * Ferdinand's most important question (*prime request*), given added weight by coming at the end of the speech, is whether or not Miranda is a *maid* (i.e. mortal girl, not immortal goddess). By calling her *wonder* he is, without knowing it, paraphrasing her name, Miranda.

But doth suffer a sea-change
Into something rich and strange.
Sea-nymphs hourly ring his knell:
        [Burden] Ding-dong.
    Hark! now I hear them – Ding-dong bell.   405

Ferdinand
The ditty does remember my drown'd father.
This is no mortal business, nor no sound
That the earth owes. I hear it now above me.

Prospero
The fringed curtains of thine eye advance,
And say what thou seest yond.

Miranda   What is't? a spirit?   410
Lord, how it looks about! Believe me, sir,
It carries a brave form. But 'tis a spirit.

Prospero
No, wench; it eats and sleeps and hath such senses
As we have, such. This gallant which thou seest
Was in the wreck; and but he's something stain'd   415
With grief, that's beauty's canker, thou mightst call
    him
A goodly person. He hath lost his fellows,
And strays about to find 'em.

Miranda   I might call him
A thing divine; for nothing natural
I ever saw so noble.

Prospero [Aside]   It goes on, I see,   420
As my soul prompts it. Spirit, fine spirit! I'll free thee
Within two days for this.

Ferdinand   Most sure, the goddess
On whom these airs attend! Vouchsafe my pray'r
May know if you remain upon this island;
And that you will some good instruction give   425
How I may bear me here. My prime request,
Which I do last pronounce, is, O you wonder!
If you be maid or no?

Miranda   No wonder, sir;

429. a maid (a) a maiden, i.e. unmarried, (b) a virgin.

430. this speech this language.

431. * **Were I ... 'tis spoken** the sense of being on an island, remote in time and place, is increased by constant references to the distant world across the sea.

431. the best? i.e. the King?

433. single alone and helpless.

433. wonders is amazed.

434. He does hear me Ferdinand is saying that since he is now the King of Naples, and can hear himself speaking, it follows that the King of Naples does hear him.

436. * **mine eyes ... ebb** Ferdinand uses a sea-image to describe his weeping. His eyes have been at high tide, flooded with tears ever since he saw his father drowned.

438. Duke of Milan i.e. Antonio. Just as Ferdinand does not know that he is *not* the King of Naples (because his father is still alive), so he does not know that Antonio is *not* the Duke of Milan (because Prospero is still alive). These are good examples of dramatic irony.

439. his brave son 'his excellent son'. We hear nothing more of Antonio having a son; perhaps he was sailing in one of the other vessels in the fleet (now *bound sadly for Naples*) and is presumed lost by Ferdinand.

440. more braver the use of a double comparative is quite common in Shakespeare.

440. control contradict.

442. chang'd eyes literally 'exchanged eyes' from gazing so fixedly at each other in their 'love at first sight' meeting. There may also be a sense of exchanging love-tokens.

444–5. * Prospero is 'playing the heavy father' and speaking with irony. He speaks *ungently*, i.e. harshly, in a discourteous fashion.

444–5. done yourself some wrong made a mistake.

448. * **To be ... way** i.e. may compassion urge my father to bend in my direction, sympathize with my feelings.

449. affection not gone forth if you haven't given your heart to anyone already.

450. Soft, sir just a moment, not so fast.

451–3. * **but this ... light** but I must make the rapid development of their feelings towards one another less easy, in case by winning each other too easily they do not value each other highly enough.

454. attend listen to, pay attention to.

454. usurp assume, take.

454. ow'st not do not own, is not rightly yours.. (Prospero is accusing Ferdinand of committing the same sins as the older generation.)

But certainly a maid.
Ferdinand   My language? Heavens!
I am the best of them that speak this speech,   430
Were I but where 'tis spoken.
Prospero   How? the best?
What wert thou, if the King of Naples heard thee?
Ferdinand
  A single thing, as I am now, that wonders
  To hear thee speak of Naples. He does hear me;
  And that he does I weep. Myself am Naples,   435
  Who with mine eyes, never since at ebb, beheld
  The King my father wreck'd.
Miranda   Alack, for mercy!
Ferdinand
  Yes, faith, and all his lords, the Duke of Milan
  And his brave son being twain.
Prospero [Aside]   The Duke of Milan
  And his more braver daughter could control thee,   440
  If now 'twere fit to do't. At the first sight
  They have chang'd eyes. Delicate Ariel,
  I'll set thee free for this. [To Ferdinand] A word,
      good sir;
  I fear you have done yourself some wrong; a word.
Miranda
  Why speaks my father so ungently? This   445
  Is the third man that e'er I saw; the first
  That e'er I sigh'd for. Pity move my father
  To be inclin'd my way!
Ferdinand   O, if a virgin,
  And your affection not gone forth, I'll make you
  The Queen of Naples.
Prospero   Soft, sir! one word more.   450
  [Aside] They are both in either's pow'rs; but this
  swift business
  I must uneasy make, lest too light winning
  Make the prize light. [To Ferdinand] One word
  more; I charge thee

458–60. * Miranda is here expressing the idea, popular in the thought of Shakespeare's time, that (a) anyone with such a handsome exterior as Ferdinand must be spiritualy good, (b) that even if the Devil (evil) did inhabit such a body (*temple*), Good would nevertheless do all it could to live there as well (i.e. in its rightful dwelling place). And so, because Good and Evil are incompatible, Evil would not be able to live together with Good in a handsome body.

461. a traitor treacherous.

462–5. manacle etc to test Ferdinand's manhood, Prospero threatens to treat him as a mutinous common sailor rather than as a prince.

466. such entertainment such treatment, such a reception.

468–9. * **Make not ... fearful** don't judge him too hastily; he's of noble birth and breeding, and no coward (i.e. he will naturally resist by drawing his sword).

470. My foot my tutor? i.e. 'Are you, my inferior, telling me what to do?' (This rebuke gains vividness if Miranda is on her knees at his feet.)

470. Put thy sword up sheathe your sword.

472. possess'd seized.

472. thy ward your 'on guard' position.

473–4. * **For ... drop** Ferdinand's sword is still drawn, and Prospero probably says what he can do rather than does it.

475–82. * Ferdinand has been tested by Prospero and shown himself so far to be resolute. Miranda's feelings are now being tried by Prospero's appearance of contemptuous brusqueness, and at the same time being strengthened.

476. surety security, bail.

That thou attend me; thou dost here usurp
The name thou ow'st not; and hast put thyself   455
Upon this island as a spy, to win it
From me, the lord on't.
Ferdinand   No, as I am a man.
Miranda
There's nothing ill can dwell in such a temple.
If the ill spirit have so fair a house,
Good things will strive to dwell with't.
Prospero   Follow me.   460
Speak not you for him; he's a traitor. Come;
I'll manacle thy neck and feet together.
Sea-water shalt thou drink; thy food shall be
The fresh-brook mussels, wither'd roots, and husks
Wherein the acorn cradled. Follow.
Ferdinand   No;   465
I will resist such entertainment till
Mine enemy has more power.

[He draws, and is charmed from moving]

Miranda   O dear father,
Make not too rash a trial of him, for
He's gentle, and not fearful.
Prospero   What, I say,
My foot my tutor? Put thy sword up, traitor;   470
Who mak'st a show but dar'st not strike, thy
          conscience
Is so possess'd with guilt. Come from thy ward;
For I can here disarm thee with this stick
And make thy weapon drop.
Miranda   Beseech you, father!
Prospero
Hence! Hang not on my garments.
Miranda   Sir, have pity;   475
I'll be his surety.
Prospero   Silence! One word more
Shall make me chide thee, if not hate thee. What!

478. * advocate ... impostor a lawyer to defend a traitor.

480. To th' most of men compared with the majority of men.

482. affections wishes, inclinations.

484. obey perhaps it is at this moment that Ferdinand sheathes his sword.

485. * Thy nerves ... in them 'your sinews are as weak as when you were an infant, and have no strength in them' (i.e. to wield a sword).

487. * My spirits ... bound up Ferdinand describes the feeling of helplessness experienced in dreams, when one is unable to perform some action (e.g. running away). In *bound up* there is another example of binding before later release.
490. subdu'd subjected, made subservient.
490. light trivial.
491. through my prison from my prison window.
492–4. * All corners ... prison let those who are free make use of the rest of the world, to its remotest extremities; I shall need no more room than my prison provides.
494. It works i.e. my plan. Whatever Prospero does to discourage Ferdinand only serves to increase his devotion, as Prospero hoped it would.

498. unwonted unusual, unaccustomed.
501. points smallest details.
501. to th' syllable exactly, to the letter.
502. Speak not for him don't try to plead for him.

By the end of Act I the introductory phase of the play is complete: characters, general situation (i.e. the tempest and what has led to it), setting and themes have all been established and Prospero, who dominates Act I, now retires into the background to allow three particular situations to develop, before moving into the foreground again in Acts IV and V. The three situations are the Ferdinand-Miranda love story, the plot by Sebastian and Antonio to murder Alonso, and the parallel plot by Caliban, Stephano and Trinculo to murder Prospero. The first of these situations has already developed by the end of Act I and reaches its climax when Ferdinand and Miranda next appear in Act III, Scene i, at the turning point of the play.

An advocate for an impostor! hush!
Thou think'st there is no more such shapes as he,
Having seen but him and Caliban. Foolish wench!   480
To th' most of men this is a Caliban,
And they to him are angels.

Miranda   My affections
Are then most humble; I have no ambition
To see a goodlier man.

Prospero   Come on; obey.
Thy nerves are in their infancy again,   485
And have no vigour in them.

Ferdinand
                     So they are;
My spirits, as in a dream, are all bound up.
My father's loss, the weakness which I feel,
The wreck of all my friends, nor this man's threats
To whom I am subdu'd, are but light to me,   490
Might I but through my prison once a day
Behold this maid. All corners else o' th' earth
Let liberty make use of; space enough
Have I in such a prison.

Prospero [Aside]
            It works. [To FERDINAND] Come on. –
Thou hast done well, fine Ariel! [To FERDINAND]
                     Follow me.   495
[To ARIEL] Hark what thou else shalt do me.

Miranda   Be of comfort;
My father's of a better nature, sir,
Than he appears by speech; this is unwonted
Which now came from him.

Prospero [To ARIEL]   Thou shalt be as free
As mountain winds; but then exactly do   500
All points of my command.

Ariel   To th' syllable.

Prospero [To FERDINAND]
Come, follow. [To MIRANDA] Speak not for him.

[Exeunt]

ACT II

Scene I

In this scene the characters of Alonso, Gonzalo, Sebastian, and Antonio, all briefly sketched in Act I, scene i, are more fully revealed. Gonzalo's loyal attempts to cheer his disconsolate king in the face of sneering cynicism by Sebastian and Antonio constitute the first half of the scene; and Sebastian and Antonio's murderous conspiracy, the second half. Prospero's island provides a 'test bed' for each character, a proving-ground in which strengths and weaknesses in personality are revealed. Gonzalo, for instance, unlike his master, Alonso, resists the temptation to despair; and Sebastian and Antonio do not resist the temptation offered by the sleeping bodies of the king and his chief counsellor.

Stage Direction. *Another part*: on the island there is little distinctive sense of location other than at Prospero's cell, and little if any scenery would have been necessary in the original production – a few property rocks and bushes at the most.

and others: nowadays most productions of the play limit Alonso's party to those named, who provide enough for a group but not enough to clutter the stage.

3–4. * **hint ... common** this sad occasion is a common enough one.

5–6. * **The masters ... woe** the owners of some merchant vessel, and the merchant himself, have precisely the same reason to be sad, (i.e. the sailor's wife awaits the return of her husband; the ship's owners, their ship; and the trader, his cargo).

8–9. * **weigh ... comfort** let the consolation of having survived outweigh (be balanced against) our reason for grief.

10–181. * Sebastian and Antonio might be sitting or standing together apart from the others, on the opposite side of the stage from Alonso and Gonzalo (who might be in the centre, and having to turn towards Sebastian and Antonio and away from the king to answer their jibes).

9–10. * **peace ... porridge** the first of many poor puns, this one plays on *peace* and pease, an ingredient in porridge.

11. * **visitor ... o'er so** the parish visitor (charitably bringing cold porridge to the sick) will not give up comforting him as easily (as the sick man gives up hope, or being comforted).

12–13. wit mind, intelligence.

12–13. strike referring to a striking or chiming watch, this suggests a return to the attack, Gonzalo trying to engage Alonso's attention.

15. One-Tell one chime has sounded – count the others.

16–17. * **When ... entertainer** if every sorrow that is presented to a person is accepted by him, then that person receives ...

ACT TWO

SCENE I. Another part of the island.

[Enter ALONSO, SEBASTIAN, ANTONIO, GONZALO,
ADRIAN, FRANCISCO, and OTHERS]

Gonzalo
  Beseech you, sir, be merry; you have cause,
  So have we all, of joy; for our escape
  Is much beyond our loss. Our hint of woe
  Is common; every day, some sailor's wife,
  The masters of some merchant, and the merchant,   5
  Have just our theme of woe; but for the miracle,
  I mean our preservation, few in millions
  Can speak like us. Then wisely, good sir, weigh
  Our sorrow with our comfort.
Alonso   Prithee, peace.
Sebastian
  He receives comfort like cold porridge.   10
Antonio
  The visitor will not give him o'er so.
Sebastian
  Look, he's winding up the watch of his wit; by and
  by it will strike.
Gonzalo
  Sir –
Sebastian
  One – Tell.   15
Gonzalo
  When every grief is entertain'd that's offer'd,
  Comes to th' entertainer –

18. dollar i.e. payment for entertainment (hospitality); a *dollar* could mean 'thaler' (a German coin) or a 'piece of eight' (a Spanish coin).

19–21. * dolour ... should Gonzalo turns away from Alonso for a moment to riposte with his pun on *dollar – dolour* (grief) and Sebastian is reduced to a sulky and ineffective reply.

23. spendthrift further play on dollar (coin), perhaps, trying to score off Gonzalo again (Gonzalo having turned back to address Alonso with *Therefore, my lord –*).

29. The old cock i.e. Gonzalo.

32. A laughter i.e. whoever loses will pay by laughing.
33. A match! done! Agreed!

35–6. * Ha, ha, ha ... paid either (a) Antonio laughs naturally, simply because he has won the bet, and Sebastian says that by laughing Antonio has paid Sebastian's debt for him, or (b) if both these lines are given to Sebastian, who has lost his wager that Gonzalo will speak first, he laughs (as the penalty) and then says that Antonio has been duly paid.

Sebastian
  A dollar.
Gonzalo
  Dolour comes to him, indeed; you have spoken
  truer than you purpos'd.   20
Sebastian
  You have taken it wiselier than I meant you should.
Gonzalo
  Therefore, my lord –
Antonio
  Fie, what a spendthrift is he of his tongue!
Alonso
  I prithee, spare.
Gonzalo
  Well, I have done; but yet –   25
Sebastian
  He will be talking.
Antonio
  Which, of he or Adrian, for a good wager, first
  begins to crow?
Sebastian
  The old cock.
Antonio
  The cock'rel.   30
Sebastian
  Done. The wager?
Antonio
  A laughter.
Sebastian
  A match!
Adrian
  Though this island seem to be desert –
Antonio
  Ha, ha, ha!   35
Sebastian
  So, you're paid.

40. he could not miss't (a) do without it (i.e. the island, or he would be in the sea), (b) miss saying it (the word *yet*).

41-2. * subtle ... temperance fine, mild and pleasant climate.

43. * Temperance ... wench Antonio perhaps hints that Temperance (moderation), a Puritan girl's name, was 'delicate' in a voluptuous rather than pure sense.

43. subtle (line 44) then follows in the derogatory sense of crafty or cunning.

44. learnedly delivered perhaps the studious (?) Adrian (*cock'rel* to the *old cock*, chip off the old block), in using long words and speaking to them deliberately, is seen as a future Gonzalo.

51. * How ... green! Gonzalo's alliterative line suggests luxuriance.

52. tawny yellow-brown. Sebastian takes a jaundiced view of the situation, and is not prepared to see anything good about it.

54-5. * He misses ... totally Antonio perhaps means that Gonzalo sees every detail, and Sebastian replies that 'he can't see the wood for the trees' (he 'miss-takes' the truth).

Adrian
  Uninhabitable, and almost inaccessible –
Sebastian
  Yet –
Adrian
  Yet –
Antonio
  He could not miss't.   40
Adrian
  It must needs be of subtle, tender, and delicate
  temperance.
Antonio
  Temperance was a delicate wench.
Sebastian
  Ay, and a subtle; as he most learnedly deliver'd.
Adrian
  The air breathes upon us here most sweetly.   45
Sebastian
  As if it had lungs, and rotten ones.
Antonio
  Or, as 'twere perfum'd by a fen.
Gonzalo
  Here is everything advantageous to life.
Antonio
  True; save means to live.
Sebastian
  Of that there's none, or little.   50
Gonzalo
  How lush and lusty the grass looks! how green!
Antonio
  The ground indeed is tawny.
Sebastian
  With an eye of green in't.
Antonio
  He misses not much.
Sebastian
  No; he doth but mistake the truth totally.   55

56. rarity marvel.
57. credit belief.
58. vouch'd claimed as true (by travellers).

61. glosses glossiness, shining newness.

63–4. * **If but ... lies?** perhaps Antonio is saying that outwardly their garments may seem as good as new, but that the truth is to be found beneath the surface (i.e. by examining a pocket). As a sneering sceptic, he won't be taken in by appearances, though in this case the appearance *is* (miraculously) the reality, which his cynicism prevents him from seeing.
65. pocket up hide away, conceal.
67. at the marriage the audience is given the reason for the sea voyage.
69–70. * **'Twas ... return** Sebastian is being sarcastic in his reference to a *sweet marriage*; and perhaps there is a dramatic irony in his use of *prosper* (i.e. little suspecting the presence of Prospero on the island).

71. such a paragon to such a perfect model for.

73–81. * Much of this passage is obscure. It becomes a little less so if we realize that there are two stories about Dido, Queen of Carthage: (a) the story in Virgil's *Aeneid* in which she became the lover of Aeneas, and (b) the story in Boccaccio in which she refused a succession of suitors. In both stories she is a widow, and in both she cremates herself: in (a) because Aeneas abandons her, and in (b) to avoid being forced into a second marriage (thus proving her faithfulness to her dead husband). Gonzalo is thinking of story (b) and Antonio of (a): for Gonzalo, therefore, Dido is a paragon of virtue, for Antonio she is an unfaithful widow, false to her husband's memory.

Gonzalo

But the rarity of it is, which is indeed almost beyond credit –

Sebastian

As many vouch'd rarities are.

Gonzalo

That our garments, being, as they were, drench'd in the sea, hold, notwithstanding, their freshness and glosses, being rather new-dy'd, than stain'd with salt water.   60

Antonio

If but one of his pockets could speak, would it not say he lies?

Sebastian

Ay, or very falsely pocket up his report.   65

Gonzalo

Methinks our garments are now as fresh as when we put them on first in Afric, at the marriage of the King's fair daughter Claribel to the King of Tunis.

Sebastian

'Twas a sweet marriage, and we prosper well in our return.   70

Adrian

Tunis was never grac'd before with such a paragon to their queen.

Gonzalo

Not since widow Dido's time.

Antonio

Widow! a pox o' that! How came that 'widow' in? Widow Dido!   75

Sebastian

What if he had said 'widower Æneas' too? Good Lord, how you take it!

Adrian

'Widow Dido' said you? You make me study of that. She was of Carthage, not of Tunis.

80–2. * Gonzalo mistakenly thinks that Tunis stands on the site of Carthage (whereas the ruins of the ancient city stand not far from Tunis), and Antonio scornfully says that he has raised a whole city and not (as Amphion did with his harp) only the walls (of Thebes).

85. * **What..next?** further dramatic irony: Antonio little realizes that although Gonzalo may not be a magician, Prospero is already making an *impossible matter* easy.

90. Ay Gonzalo is probably re-affirming line 80, conversing with Adrian during lines 81–7, and Antonio takes it that he is agreeing to the comic exaggerations about islands and apples.
91. in good time at last! (i.e. at last Gonzalo has responded).

95. * **And ... there** a mocking echo of line 69.
96. * **Bate ... Dido** with the exception of widow Dido, please.
97. * **O ... Ay ... Dido** some rhyme effect is suggested here, e.g. 'widow Dido'.
98. doublet close-fitting garment, with or without sleeves, worn as a tunic over a shirt and under a longer outer garment or short cloak.

99. in a sort more or less, after a fashion.
100. * **That ... fish'd for** you took your time to land that fish, i.e. to make that qualification (that your doublet was only more or less as fresh as when you first wore it). Gonzalo *first wore* it at the wedding presumably because it had been specially made for the royal wedding.

Gonzalo
This Tunis, sir, was Carthage.   80
Adrian
Carthage?
Gonzalo
I assure you, Carthage.
Antonio
His word is more than the miraculous harp.
Sebastian
He hath rais'd the wall, and houses too.
Antonio
What impossible matter will he make easy next?   85
Sebastian
I think he will carry this island home in his pocket,
and give it his son for an apple.
Antonio
And, sowing the kernels of it in the sea, bring forth
more islands.
Gonzalo
Ay.   90
Antonio
Why, in good time.
Gonzalo
Sir, we were talking that our garments seem now as
fresh as when we were at Tunis at the marriage of
your daughter, who is now Queen.
Antonio
And the rarest that e'er came there.   95
Sebastian
Bate, I beseech you, widow Dido.
Antonio
O, widow Dido! Ay, widow Dido.
Gonzalo
Is not, sir, my doublet as fresh as the first day I
wore it? I mean, in a sort.
Antonio
That 'sort' was well fish'd for.   100

102–3. * **You cram … sense** Alonso is sick of being reminded of the wedding, the result of which is that he has lost both his children. The image is of force-feeding: as his hearing (*sense*) is crammed with unpalatable words, he is sickened by them.

105. rate estimation.

107–8. * **O thou … Milan** presumably as part of the deal with Alonso, Antonio has agreed to Ferdinand's inheriting the Dukedom of Milan rather than his own son. It is ironical that Ferdinand, in marrying Miranda, will in fact rule both Naples and Milan.

108. strange foreign.

109–18. * This is Francisco's only speech in the play, and some editors give it to Gonzalo. He gives an heroic picture of Ferdinand battling his way ashore.

109–18. beat, ride, trod, enmity, bold, lusty stroke all give an impression of a champion in battle, in single fight against a whole army.

109–18. surge most swoln mountainous wave (like an advancing rank of soldiers).

109–18. contentious waves challenging waves (of troops).

116–117. * **To th' shore … him** the overhanging cliffs (or perhaps concave sand-dunes) are pictured as leaning to help him ashore.

116–17. his its.

116–17. basis foot (i.e. beach). The image may continue the battle idea: the land (Ferdinand's ally) is like a friendly soldier coming to the aid of the hero struck down in the fight.

119–21. * **loss … bless … lose** the verbs gain emphasis from the 'l' and 's' alliterations. *Lose* repeats *loss*, but is also *loose* (release), a term used to describe the releasing of a mare to mate with a stallion, and would express Sebastian's disgust at Alonso's allowing the *fair soul* (line 125) to marry a dark-skinned African.

122–3. * **Where … on't** where (i.e. in Africa) she, to say the least, is banished from you (i.e. like a traitor rather than your loving daugher), who have good reason to weep over your grievous loss.

126. * **Weigh'd … obedience** undecided (*weigh'd* in the balance) whether to refuse (*loathness:* reluctance) or to obey.

127. * **Which … bow** which end of the scales should descend (i.e. which side to come down on, that of her inclination not to marry the African or that of obedience to her father).

129. Moe more.

129. of this business' making as the result of this wedding. (Sebastian's bitter use of *business* suggests a purely political marriage.)

Gonzalo
　When I wore it at your daughter's marriage?
Alonso
　You cram these words into mine ears against
　The stomach of my sense. Would I had never
　Married my daughter there; for, coming thence,
　My son is lost; and, in my rate, she too,　　　　105
　Who is so far from Italy removed
　I ne'er again shall see her. O thou mine heir
　Of Naples and of Milan, what strange fish
　Hath made his meal on thee?
Francisco　　　　　　　　　　Sir, he may live;
　I saw him beat the surges under him,　　　　110
　And ride upon their backs; he trod the water,
　Whose enmity he flung aside, and breasted
　The surge most swoln that met him; his bold head
　'Bove the contentious waves he kept, and oared
　Himself with his good arms in lusty stroke　　115
　To th' shore, that o'er his wave-worn basis bowed,
　As stooping to relieve him. I not doubt
　He came alive to land.
Alonso　　　　　　　　No, no, he's gone.
Sebastian
　Sir, you may thank yourself for this great loss,
　That would not bless our Europe with your daughter,　120
　But rather lose her to an African;
　Where she, at least, is banish'd from your eye,
　Who hath cause to wet the grief on't.
Alonso　　　　　　　　　　Prithee, peace.
Sebastian
　You were kneel'd to, and importun'd otherwise
　By all of us; and the fair soul herself　　　　125
　Weigh'd between loathness and obedience at
　Which end o' th' beam should bow. We have lost
　　　your son,
　I fear, for ever. Milan and Naples have
　Moe widows in them of this business' making,

130. * Than ... them Sebastian assumes that the whole fleet has been lost and that he and his companions are the sole survivors.

131. * So is ... loss so is the keenest feeling of loss.

134. time the right moment, suitable occasion.

136. chirurgeonly like a good surgeon.

137–8. * It is ... cloudy Gonzalo says that they are all depressed when the king is gloomy (overcast). The image of the king as the sun, here behind the clouds, and like them 'heavy' with weeping rain, is common in Shakespeare. In the metaphor there is perhaps an echo of the tempest weather.

138. Fowl a pun (perhaps obscure, perhaps feeble) on *foul*. There may be a connection with *the old cock* (line 29).

139. plantation colonization, colonizing of. Gonzalo's meaning is deliberately misunderstood as 'planting' by Antonio.

140. nettle-seed etc i.e. weeds.

142. want lack. (Sebastian's remark anticipates 'king' Stephano's butt of wine in Act II, Scene ii; presumably he is thirsty and could do with a drink of wine at this moment.)

143–63. * Gonzalo's description of an ideal (if impracticable) commonwealth is probably derived from Montaigne's essay on cannibals, which was pulished in Florio's English translation in 1603.

143–4. * I' th' commonwealth ... things in my ideal society I would see that everything was carried out in exactly the opposite manner to what is customary (in normal societies).

144–5. * no ... admit I would permit no trade of any kind.

144–5. name of magistrate title of magistrate (i.e. no one would be called 'magistrate').

146. letters learning, literacy.

147. use of service employing, and being employed as, servants.

147. succession inheritance.

148. Bourn boundary.

148. tilth tillage, ploughed land.

149. * no use ... oil i.e. because these are all examples of man's use of raw materials not being used by him in their raw state. *metal* comes from ore, *corn* has to be ground in a mill, *wine* pressed from grapes and *oil* from olives.

152–3. * Sebastian and Antonio miss the point of Gonzalo's words by taking what he says too literally: he is theorizing rather than offering practical advice, and is also stil trying to take Alonso's mind off the wreck. He may also be making deliberate mistakes in order to *minister occasion* (line 166) to *these gentlemen*.

Than we bring men to comfort them;   130
The fault's your own.
Alonso   So is the dear'st o' th' loss.
Gonzalo
My lord Sebastian,
The truth you speak doth lack some gentleness,
And time to speak it in; you rub the sore,
When you should bring the plaster.
Sebastian   Very well.   135
Antonio
And most chirurgeonly.
Gonzalo
It is foul weather in us all, good sir,
When you are cloudy.
Sebastian   Fowl weather?
Antonio   Very foul.
Gonzalo
Had I plantation of this isle, my lord –
Antonio
He'd sow 't with nettle-seed.
Sebastian   Or docks, or mallows.   140
Gonzalo
And were the king on't, what would I do?
Sebastian
Scape being drunk for want of wine.
Gonzalo
I' th' commonwealth I would by contraries
Execute all things; for no kind of traffic
Would I admit; no name of magistrate;   145
Letters should not be known; riches, poverty,
And use of service, none; contract, succession,
Bourn, bound of land, tilth, vineyard, none;
No use of metal, corn or wine, or oil;
No occupation; all men idle, all;   150
And women too, but innocent and pure;
No sovereignty –

155–6. Treason, felony, sword all three words are appropriate to the actions of Sebastian and Antonio later in the scene.

156. engine instrument or machine of war (or perhaps torture, e.g. the rack, if taken with *treason, felony*, for which crimes torture would be the punishment before execution; Montaigne says that it is worse 'to mangle by tortures and torments' a living body than to eat a dead one, in his essay on cannibals).

157. bring forth bear, produce.

157. Of its own kind of itself, without man's help.

158. foison plenty.

161. all idle Antonio scornfully repeats Gonzalo's words (line 148) and suggests that in the commonwealth of 'contraries', marriage, demanding hard work, will be replaced by purely lustful couplings between sluts and menservants (which, becaue everyone is equal and there are no classes in the commonwealth where everything is 'in common', is the level to which everyone will descend).

163. Save God save.

166. minister occasion provide an opportunity.

167. sensible sensitive.

168. use are accustomed.

Sebastian　　　　　　Yet he would be king on't.
Antonio
　The latter end of his commonwealth forgets the
　　　beginning.
Gonzalo
　All things in common nature should produce
　Without sweat or endeavour. Treason, felony,　　　　155
　Sword, pike, knife, gun, or need of any engine,
　Would I not have; but nature should bring forth,
　Of it own kind, all foison, all abundance,
　To feed my innocent people.
Sebastian
　No marrying 'mong his subjects?　　　　　　160
Antonio
　None, man; all idle; whores and knaves.
Gonzalo
　I would with such perfection govern, sir,
　T' excel the golden age.
Sebastian　　　　　　Save his Majesty!
Antonio
　Long live Gonzalo!
Gonzalo　　　　　　And – do you mark me, sir?
Alonso
　Prithee, no more; thou dost talk nothing to me.　　　　165
Gonzalo
　I do well believe your Highness; and did it to
　minister occasion to these gentlemen, who are of
　such sensible and nimble lungs that they always use
　to laugh at nothing.
Antonio
　'Twas you we laugh'd at.　　　　　　170
Gonzalo
　Who in this kind of merry fooling am nothing to
　you; so you may continue, and laugh at nothing still.
Antonio
　What a blow was there given!

174. An if.

174. flat-long with the flat of the blade (i.e it wasn't a cutting remark).

175. brave mettle fine spirit. Gonzalo uses *brave* ironically, and in *mettle* (metal) continues the image of a sword in *blow* and *flat-long*. After this verbal fencing, real swords will be drawn (line 288).

175–7. * you would ... changing in the Ptolemaic system of astronomy, still used in Shakespeare's time, the seven planets, of which the Moon was closest to the Earth, revolved in their spheres or orbits around the Earth, which was stationary at the centre of the whole system or 'World' (Universe). Gonzalo says that if the Moon remained unchanged, at the full, for more than a month, they (Sebastian and Antonio) would in their lunacy try to perform the impossible (i.e. lift it out of its natural course).

Stage Direction. **Ariel, invisible, playing** perhaps Ariel, whose soothing, slow music is as inaudible to the characters as he is invisible, shows his selection of those he wishes to put to sleep by standing by them as he plays, each in turn. The stately 'air' provides a change of key in the dialogue and introduces the sinister 'sleepy language' of the treacherous plotting.

178. * We would ... a-bat-fowling we would use the moon as a lantern (i.e. having taken it from its sphere) to attract roosting birds and then knock them down with sticks and clubs. Sebastian may also be referring to 'gulling' or tricking Gonzalo (with echoes, perhaps of *cock* and *fowl*).

179. * Nay ... angry perhaps this is in response to some gesture (hand on sword-hilt) of Gonzalo's, or possibly to provoke him further.

180–1. * No I ... weakly no, I assure you, I won't lose my temper over a triviality.

181–2. * Will you ... heavy? will you continue your feeble jokes until I yawn and fall asleep, for I am feeling very sleepy?

183. * Go ... hear us lie down, and listen to our laughter.

185. with themselves by closing their lids.

186. inclin'd being persuaded (by weariness pushing them in that direction).

187. omit disregard, ignore.

187. heavy sleepy.

191. watch your safety keep awake to guard your safety.

Sebastian
  An it had not fall'n flat-long.
Gonzalo
  You are gentlemen of brave mettle; you would lift   175
  the moon out of her sphere, if she would continue
  in it five weeks without changing.

  [Enter ARIEL, invisible, playing solemn music]

Sebastian
  We would so, and then go a-bat-fowling.
Antonio
  Nay, good my lord, be not angry.
Gonzalo
  No, I warrant you; I will not adventure my   180
  discretion so weakly. Will you laugh me asleep, for I
  am very heavy?
Antonio
  Go sleep, and hear us.

  [All sleep but ALONSO, SEBASTIAN and ANTONIO]

Alonso
  What, all so soon asleep! I wish mine eyes
  Would, with themselves, shut up my thoughts; I find   185
  They are inclin'd to do so.
Sebastian   Please you, sir,
  Do not omit the heavy offer of it:
  It seldom visits sorrow; when it doth,
  It is a comforter.
Antonio   We two, my lord,
  Will guard your person while you take your rest,   190
  And watch your safety.
Alonso
  Thank you – wondrous heavy!

            [ALONSO sleeps.
            Exit ARIEL]

194. quality see Act I, Scene ii, line 337.

196. my spirits are nimble I'm wide awake, my mind is alert.

198. thunderstroke as if struck by lightning.

201. th' occasion speaks thee the opportunity invites you (to make use of it).

202. * **My strong ... sees** my imagination is strongly convinced that it sees.

203. waking awake.

205. sleepy language i.e. words such as you might hear in a dream. (The repetition of 'sleep' and 's' alliterations gives the feelings of soft drowsiness.) The sleep-walking picture painted by Sebastian is strongly reminiscent in its language of *Macbeth* Act V, Scene i, lines 6–8.

210–11. * **wink'st ... waking** i.e. you are going around with your eyes shut (to your opportunities).

211. distinctly i.e. it is possible to distinguish a meaning in your snoring.

213. * **more ... custom** Antonio removes the mask of flippancy he has been wearing (his usual manner) to get down to brass tacks.

214. if heed me if you want to take in what I am going to say.

215. Trebles thee o'er makes you three times as great as you are now. (Perhaps Sebastian is at three removes from the throne, Alonso and his two children being in the way.)

215. standing water i.e. uncommitted, ready to be moved (like the sea, stationary for a time at high tide before it begins to ebb, or at low tide before it begins to rise).

216. flow rise (like the tide) in the world.

216–17.* **to ebb ... me** inborn idleness persuades me to sink. As Alonso's younger brother, and not in line for the crown, Sebastian would naturally lack incentive to do more than drift: Antonio was provided with an incentive by Prospero's virtual abdication, and is therefore the more positive of the two, though not necessarily the stronger character.

Sebastian
  What a strange drowsiness possesses them!
Antonio
  It is the quality o' th' climate.
Sebastian   Why
  Doth it not then our eyelids sink? I find not   195
  Myself dispos'd to sleep.
Antonio   Nor I; my spirits are nimble.
  They fell together all, as by consent;
  They dropp'd, as by a thunder-stroke. What might,
  Worthy Sebastian? O, what might! No more!
  And yet methinks I see it in thy face,   200
  What thou shouldst be; th' occasion speaks thee;
        and
  My strong imagination sees a crown
  Dropping upon thy head.
Sebastian   What, art thou waking?
Antonio
  Do you not hear me speak?
Sebastian   I do; and surely
  It is a sleepy language, and thou speak'st   205
  Out of thy sleep. What is it thou didst say?
  This is a strange repose, to be asleep
  With eyes wide open; standing, speaking, moving,
  And yet so fast asleep.
Antonio   Noble Sebastian,
  Thou let'st thy fortune sleep – die rather; wink'st   210
  Whiles thou art waking.
Sebastian   Thou dost snore distinctly;
  There's meaning in thy snores.
Antonio
  I am more serious than my custom; you
  Must be so too, if heed me; which to do
  Trebles thee o'er.
Sebastian
  Well, I am standing water.   215
Antonio
  I'll teach you how to flow.

219–21. * If you ... invest it if you could only see how much you welcome
the idea (of removing Alonso) in pretending to scorn the suggestion; how, in
ridiculing the idea, you make it appear more attractive.

219–21. Invest literally, clothe it.

221–3. * Ebbing ... sloth failures do indeed generally sink to the very bottom of society either through their lack of guts or sheer laziness. (The sea
metaphor appears again in *standing water ... ebb ... ebbing ... bottom.*)

224. setting fixed expression.

224. * proclaim ... thee tell me publicly (clearly) that you have something
important to say.

225–6. * a birth ... yield a subject which you find a good deal of difficulty
in delivering (i.e. expressing).

227. of weak remembrance with a poor memory (perhaps a sign of old
age, e.g. muddling Carthage and Tunis?).

228. as little memory as little remembered (i.e. as soon forgotten as he
himself forgets things).

229. earth'd buried. (Antonio is hinting towards the coming plot to kill
Alonso and Gonzalo.)

230–1. * he's ... persuade Gonzalo is the epitome of persuasiveness, and
his only occupation, his profession, is diplomacy. (Antonio shows himself to
be a subtle and powerful persuader of Sebastian in this scene, and is perhaps
conscious of the irony in his description of Gonzalo.)

235–8. * No hope ... there having no hope in that direction (i.e. the possibility that Ferdinand is alive) means that you have such high hopes in another direction (the throne of Naples) that even Ambition itself can do no more
than see a short distance beyond (i.e. beyond the throne), but doubts finding anything worth aiming at there (because the throne of Naples is the
highest target Ambition can aim at).

241–5. * She ... she ... she ... she the repetition becomes more and more
sarcastic and the sentences longer as Antonio delivers his scornful exaggerations, designed to rouse Sebastian from his 'sloth'.

241. Queen of Tunis rhythmically balances *heir of Naples*, and by contrast
places Claribel out of the running, i.e. she is *queen* and cannot be an *heir*, in
Tunis and therefore cannot be in *Naples*.

242. * ten ... life literally, thirty miles further than a journey which would
take a man his whole life to accomplish. (Antonio is deliberately ignoring the
fact that they have only just come from the wedding in Tunis: his language
has all the energy and brazen exaggeration of the demagogue and the confidence trickster.)

243. no note no information, news.

243. post courier.

Sebastian   Do so: to ebb,
  Hereditary sloth instructs me.
Antonio   O,
  If you but knew how you the purpose cherish,
  Whiles thus you mock it! how, in stripping it,   220
  You more invest it! Ebbing men indeed,
  Most often, do so near the bottom run
  By their own fear or sloth.
Sebastian   Prithee say on.
  The setting of thine eye and cheek proclaim
  A matter from thee; and a birth, indeed,   225
  Which throes thee much to yield.
Antonio   Thus, sir:
  Although this lord of weak remembrance, this
  Who shall be of as little memory
  When he is earth'd, hath here almost persuaded –
  For he's a spirit of persuasion, only   230
  Professes to persuade – the King his son's alive,
  'Tis as impossible that he's undrown'd
  As he that sleeps here swims.
Sebastian   I have no hope
  That he's undrown'd.
Antonio   O, out of that 'no hope'
  What great hope have you! No hope that way is   235
  Another way so high a hope, that even
  Ambition cannot pierce a wink beyond,
  But doubt discovery there. Will you grant with me
  That Ferdinand is drown'd?
Sebastian   He's gone.
Antonio   Then tell me,
  Who's the next heir of Naples?
Sebastian   Claribel.   240
Antonio
  She that is Queen of Tunis; she that dwells
  Ten leagues beyond man's life; she that from
      Naples
  Can have no note, unless the sun were post,

245. from whom coming from whom.

246. cast vomited, spewed, thrown up (on to the shore). Ariel uses the same image at Act III, Scene iii, line 56. *Cast* then suggests actors in the following lines (247–9).

246–9. * **cast … discharge** in *cast, perform, act, prologue,* and *discharge* there is a succession of theatrical terms. The *discharge*, in the sense of executing a performance (i.e. seeing that it is carried out), will be in 'producer' Prospero's hands and not Antonio's and Sebastian's, though.

250. stuff literally 'padding'. Sebastian, in his dry, cautious way, suggests that Antonio is being bombastic (bombast is cotton-wool used in padding clothes). Prospero uses the word *stuff* in Act IV, Scene i, line 156 when speaking in theatrical terms of the Masque.

253. cubit approx. twenty inches, roughly a pace or step.

255. measure us retrace us (i.e. the cubits), return step by step.

256. wake arouse himself (from the *sleep* of lines 207–8).

257. seiz'd arrested, gripped.

259–60. * **prate … amply** talk as longwindedly.

261–2. * **I … chat** Antonio either means (a) that he could be as garrulous as Gonzalo or (b) that he could train (*make*) a jackdaw (*chough*) caw (*chat*) as profoundly (*deep*) i.e. Gonzalo's talk is as empty as a jackdaw's mimicking. (The alliteration of *chough* and *chat*, and the oxymoron in *deep chat* are good examples of Antonio's verbal energy.)

265–6. * **And how … fortune** and how does your desire (*content*) regard (*tender*) this lucky chance (*good fortune*)?

268. * **And look … me** in Shakespeare, repeatedly, robes denote the ruler and disguise the usurper. (There is another reminder here of the drenching yet freshening effect of the sea.)

269. feater more trimly, neatly, gracefully (with the sense of being both worn with more confidence and being better tailored).

270. fellows see Act I, Scene ii, line 417 (note).

271. But, for your conscience but what about your conscience?

The Man i' th' Moon's too slow, till newborn chins
Be rough and razorable; she that from whom   245
We all were sea-swallow'd, though some cast again,
And by that destiny, to perform an act
Whereof what's past is prologue, what to come
In yours and my discharge.
Sebastian
What stuff is this! How say you?   250
'Tis true, my brother's daughter's Queen of Tunis;
So is she heir of Naples; 'twixt which regions
There is some space.
Antonio   A space whose ev'ry cubit
Seems to cry out 'How shall that Claribel
Measure us back to Naples? Keep in Tunis,   255
And let Sebastian wake'. Say this were death
That now hath seiz'd them; why, they were no
        worse
Than now they are. There be that can rule Naples
As well as he that sleeps; lords that can prate
As amply and unnecessarily   260
As this Gonzalo; I myself could make
A chough of as deep chat. O, that you bore
The mind that I do! What a sleep were this
For your advancement! Do you understand me?
Sebastian
Methinks I do.
Antonio
And how does your content   265
Tender your own good fortune?
Sebastian   I remember
You did supplant your brother Prospero.
Antonio
True.
And look how well my garments sit upon me,
Much feater than before. My brother's servants
Were then my fellows; now they are my men.   270
Sebastian
But, for your conscience –

272–3. * If ... slipper if it were a blister on my heel, I'd have to wear a slipper. (The matter-of-fact reply shows how easily Antonio shrugs off any feeling of remorse.)

274. * this deity ... bosom this god (conscience) ruling in my heart.

275–6. * candied ... molest may they (consciences) be no more than sugary sweets which dissolve before they prevent (me). The image is found elsewhere in Shakespeare and is associated with flattery, fawning dogs, 'sucking up', and sweets.

276. brother the repetition (lines 251, 267, 269) emphasizes the unnatural fratricide.

277–8. * No ... dead Alonso looks dead as he sleeps, and he would be no better than the earth he is lying on if he were dead. (Antonio's callous suggestion that Alonso might as well be dead is an attempt to make Sebastian only see the externals of the situation.)

279. * obedient ... of it only three inches of Antonio's trusty servant, his sword, are required to reach Alonso's heart. (Perhaps Antonio draws his sword a few inches from its scabbard and thrusts it back again at *lay to bed*.)

281. wink sleep 'shut-eye' (*perpetual wink:* death). The combination of *perpetual* and *for aye* (for ever) reinforces the conclusiveness of the action ('for ever and ever, amen').

282. morsel scrap (of food, flesh). Shakespeare often associates 'morsel' with death (which consumes the flesh, body).

282. Sir Prudence mockingly descriptive of the cautious Gonzalo, and possibly reminiscent of line 42. If so, Gonzalo (*Sir*) is an 'old maid' (*Prudence*) rather than a gallant knight (e.g. Sir Lancelot).

283. upbraid criticize, condemn.

283–6. * For ... hour i.e. the other courtiers, as ready to be tempted as a cat is to lap up milk, will agree to anything that he and Sebastian propose in the way of an explanation.

286–7. * case ... precedent Sebastian uses legal terms (*case ... precedent*) to sanction, perhaps with a sense of irony in so doing, their intended crime: i.e. 'because you have established a precedent (recognized way of proceeding) I can now follow your line of behaviour on what I shall do.'

288. come by get possession of.

290. Draw together let's unsheathe our swords simultaneously. Perhaps Antonio wants to make sure that if the king or any of his followers suddenly wake up, or should Sebastian 'double-cross' him by rousing them, he will not be the only one found with a drawn sword in his hand.

292. Gonzalo Antonio is not asking Sebastian to commit fratricide, so he will kill Alonso, while Sebastian kills Gonzalo. (Furthermore, Antonio will be quite sure if he kills Alonso personally of being free from the tribute he pays to him.)

292. O, but one word this is perhaps a rather obvious dramatic device to allow Ariel time to rouse Gonzalo, and, if they withdraw to the rear of the stage, or to one side, space for him to move in.

294. his friend i.e. Gonzalo (see Act I, Scene ii, lines 161–2). Ariel is here speaking to the audience, addressing Gonzalo impersonally and telling the audience that he has come to keep *them* (Alonso and Gonzalo) alive.

Antonio
 Ay, sir; where lies that? If 'twere a kibe,
 'Twould put me to my slipper; but I feel not
 This deity in my bosom; twenty consciences
 That stand 'twixt me and Milan, candied be they   275
 And melt, ere they molest! Here lies your brother,
 No better than the earth he lies upon,
 If he were that which now he's like – that's dead;
 Whom I with this obedient steel, three inches of it,
 Can lay to bed for ever; whiles you, doing thus,   280
 To the perpetual wink for aye might put
 This ancient morsel, this Sir Prudence, who
 Should not upbraid our course. For all the rest,
 They'll take suggestion as a cat laps milk;
 They'll tell the clock to any business that   285
 We say befits the hour.
Sebastian   Thy case, dear friend,
 Shall be my precedent; as thou got'st Milan,
 I'll come by Naples. Draw thy sword. One stroke
 Shall free thee from the tribute which thou payest;
 And I the King shall love thee.
Antonio   Draw together;   290
 And when I rear my hand, do you the like,
 To fall it on Gonzalo.
Sebastian   O, but one word.

     [They talk apart]
   [Re-enter ARIEL, invisible, with music and song]

Ariel
 My master through his art foresees the danger
 That you, his friend, are in; and sends me forth –

295. project see note to Act V, Scene i, line 1.
295. project dies plan is ruined, purpose fails.
296. snoring i.e. in exhausted sleep.
297. open-ey'd conspiracy traitors who are awake.

298. * **His ... take** seizes his opportunity.

302. sudden swift, speedy.

303. Preserve the King! loyal Gonzalo's first thought is for his master's safety.
305. ghastly looking Antonio and Sebastian are pale and grim-faced (like ghosts), presumably with a combination of horror and determination at the thought of committing a cold-blooded murder, but may also be aghast at being discovered with swords drawn. Is Alonso suspicious?
306–9. * It is interesting that it is Sebastian rather than the previously more voluble Antonio who speaks first; perhaps he is the 'cooler customer' of the two. On the other hand, it may simply be that he is standing over Gonzalo, about to kill him, and therefore replies to him.
307. hollow echoing, reverberating. *Hollow* can also mean false, which is what the fictitious *bellowing* was.
310. din although Sebastian and Antonio are inventing noises of wild beasts to explain away their drawn swords, travellers' tales of the period mention terrifying sounds being heard on unexplored islands. It is ironical that Prospero's island is in fact *full of noises*, as Caliban says (Act III, Scene ii, line 131).
310. monster's a monster is an unnatural creature, and not necessarily a large one. The indirect suggestion here is that even the monster Caliban would have been frightened (and he shows no fear of strange noises in Act III, Scene ii, line 131); and it is ironical that Antonio (who perhaps replies to Alonso because he is standing over *him*) is himself a monster of unnaturalness as a potential murderer.
313. humming i.e. Ariel's song (compare Act III, Scene ii, line 134).
315. cried cried out.

For else his project dies – to keep them living.   295

        [Sings in Gonzalo's ear]

    While you here do snoring lie,
      Open-ey'd conspiracy
    His time doth take.
      If of life you keep a care,
    Shake off slumber, and beware.   300
    Awake, awake!

Antonio

Then let us both be sudden.

Gonzalo   Now, good angels
Preserve the King!

        [They wake]

Alonso

Why, how now? – Ho, awake! – Why are you drawn?
Wherefore this ghastly looking?

Gonzalo   What's the matter?   305

Sebastian

Whiles we stood here securing your repose,
Even now, we heard a hollow burst of bellowing
Like bulls, or rather lions; did't not wake you?
It struck mine ear most terribly.

Alonso   I heard nothing.

Antonio

O, 'twas a din to fright a monster's ear,   310
To make an earthquake! Sure it was the roar
Of a whole herd of lions.

Alonso   Heard you this, Gonzalo?

Gonzalo

Upon mine honour, sir, I heard a humming,
And that a strange one too, which did awake me;
I shak'd you, sir, and cried; as mine eyes open'd,   315
I saw their weapons drawn – there was a noise,
That's verily. 'Tis best we stand upon our guard,
Or that we quit this place. Let's draw our weapons.

320. * Heavens ... beasts Gonzalo may suspect Sebastian and Antonio, in which case *beasts* refers to them; even if he does not, it can refer to them through an unconscious irony on Gonzalo's part.

By the end of this scene we have begun to sympathize a little with Alonso, because of his suffering in the supposed loss of his son and the plot on his life: he is ripe for repentance and forgiveness. Antonio and Sebastian, in contrast, have increased in guilt. All *three men of sin*, when they next appear (in Act III, scene iii), reach the turning point of their part of the play's action when they recognise their guilt and have an opportunity of redeeming the past by repentance.

SCENE II

The third situation is now developed when Caliban meets Trinculo, the royal jester, and Stephano, the royal butler. They form a comic counterpart to the *three men of sin* (Alonso, Sebastian and Antonio), and like them are tempted to conspiracy. The clowning gives the audience an opportunity to relax and laugh, though as always in Shakespeare's plays the comedy is used to mirror the main action and intensify its meaning.

Stage Direction. **burden of wood** the opening of this scene is identical with that of Act III, Scene i, with the parallel, log-bearing situation underlining the contrast between Caliban and Ferdinand, and yet also indicating their common characteristics: they are both men, though each stands at a different end of the human scale.

2. flats swamps. (The expletive force of *fens, flats, fall* is considerable; as Caliban has said, his profit from learning language is that he knows how to curse.)
3. inch-meal inch by inch, measured in inches (*meal*: measure).
5. urchin-shows hobgoblin apparitions.
5. pitch throw, toss (with perhaps a play on *pitch* tar, i.e. he will be defiled by being pitched into the mud).
6. firebrand flaming torch (here, will o' th' wisp, leading him astray into swamps). There is a suggestion of Ariel in this: he *flam'd amazement* on board ship, and in Act IV, Scene i, line 182 decribes leading Caliban and the others into the *filthy mantled pool*; though then by means of music.
9. mow grimace (mockingly).
11. tumbling rolling.
11. mount raise.
12. pricks prickles, spikes.
13. wound entwined with, wound round with.
Stage Direction. **Trinculo** as the King's Jester, dressed probably in his motley (parti-coloured costume), wet, shivering, and scared of being the only survivor. Caliban mistakes him for one of Prospero's spirits because of his strange appearance.
15. and to in order to.

Alonso
    Lead off this ground; and let's make further search
    For my poor son.
Gonzalo   Heavens keep him from these beasts!   320
    For he is, sure, i' th' island.
Alonso   Lead away.
Ariel
    Prospero my lord shall know what I have done;
    So, King, go safely on to seek thy son.

              [Exeunt]

      SCENE II. Another part of the island.

     [Enter CALIBAN, with a burden of wood.
         A noise of thunder heard]

Caliban
    All the infections that the sun sucks up
    From bogs, fens, flats, on Prosper fall, and make
       him
    By inch-meal a disease! His spirits hear me,
    And yet I needs must curse. But they'll nor pinch,
    Fright me with urchin-shows, pitch me i' th' mire,   5
    Nor lead me, like a firebrand, in the dark
    Out of my way, unless he bid 'em; but
    For every trifle are they set upon me;
    Sometime like apes that mow and chatter at me,
    And after bite me; then like hedgehogs which   10
    Lie tumbling in my barefoot way, and mount
    Their pricks at my footfall; sometime am I
    All wound with adders, who with cloven tongues
    Do hiss me into madness.

            [Enter TRINCULO]

              Lo, now, lo!
    Here comes a spirit of his, and to torment me   15

17. mind notice.

18. * Stephano and Trinculo speak in prose, in the usual Shakespearean convention for comic characters or the common people. Caliban (perhaps because he has learnt a nobler form of speech from Prospero and Miranda) by contrast, speaks in verse, and even in prose conversation has a rhythmical dignity and power in his language which distinguishes him from the two 'clowns'.

18. bear off keep off, ward off.

18. weather storm, tempest.

19. brewing being prepared (suggesting *liquor* in line 21, which in turn anticipates Stephano's bottle of sack).

21. foul bombard (a) a large leathern jug, (b) a siege cannon. Both meanings are present here: the black cloud is about to empty its contents, and the thunder cloud to roar out (compare descriptions of the tempest in Act I). It is *foul* because it is discharging 'dirty weather'.

21. shed his liquor i.e. the black cloud will empty its contents (rain). There may also be a suggestion either of vomiting or urinating; Trinculo's humour is repeatedly foul-minded (compare *backward voice*, line 90, *siege*, line 104, and *vent*, line 104).

26–7. * **a kind of ... Poor-John** a sort of decidedly not at all fresh dried hake (i.e. with a very unpleasant smell).

27. A strange fish! an odd creature! Caliban may smell like a fish but does not look like one. Having just survived drowning, Trinculo may have his mind filled with fish; probably he simply means something like, 'How strange!' Compare the modern expression 'fishy' for 'strange' or 'suspicious'.

28. painted i.e. a painted booth-sign at a fair to attract the curious to 'walk up' and see the 'strange fish', the novelty brought back from a distant land.

29. piece of silver i.e. more than a mere copper coin.

29. monster make a man (a) make a man's fortune, (b) be taken for a man (pass as one).

31–2. give a doit give a farthing, give a sou. (A doit was a small Dutch coin of low value.)

31–2. lay out spend.

33. Indian an inhabitant of the New World. Many were brought to Europe in Shakespeare's time to be exhibited as curiosities, and few survived their contact with civilization. (Trinculo suggests in line 27 that he would make a great profit from Caliban in England, the sort of joke against themselves that English audiences enjoy.)

33–4. * **his fins ... arms** This does not mean that Caliban's arms look like fins, but simply that Trinculo, expecting to find fins on his fish, is surprised to find arms instead.

33–4. Warm i.e. unlike a cold-blooded fish.

34. let loose express. Perhaps like Jove loosing a thunderbolt, and possibly, together with *hold it no longer* (line 35), meaning to fart (see note to line 21).

38. gaberdine cloak.

39–40. * **Misery ... bedfellow** a proverbial saying. (The meaning is: 'when you are down on your luck, you may have to lay your head anywhere'.)

40. shroud shelter, take cover.

40. dregs i.e. the last drops of the 'foul bombard'.

For bringing wood in slowly. I'll fall flat;
Perchance he will not mind me.

Trinculo

Here's neither bush nor shrub to bear off any
weather at all, and another storm brewing; I hear it
sing i' th' wind. Yond same black cloud, yond huge   20
one, looks like a foul bombard that would shed his
liquor. If it should thunder as it did before, I know
not where to hide my head. Yond same cloud
cannot choose but fall by pailfuls. What have we
here? a man or a fish? dead or alive? A fish: he   25
smells like a fish; a very ancient and fish-like smell;
a kind of not-of-the-newest Poor-John. A strange
fish! Were I in England now, as once I was, and had
but this fish painted, not a holiday fool there but
would give a piece of silver. There would this   30
monster make a man; any strange beast there
makes a man; when they will not give a doit to
relieve a lame beggar, they will lay out ten to see a
dead Indian. Legg'd like a man, and his fins like
arms! Warm, o' my troth! I do now let loose my
opinion; hold it no longer: this is no fish, but an   35
islander, that hath lately suffered by a thunderbolt.
[Thunder] Alas, the storm is come again! My best
way is to creep under his gaberdine; there is no
other shelter hereabout. Misery acquaints a man
with strange bedfellows. I will here shroud till the   40
dregs of the storm be past.

Stage Direction. **Enter Stephano** his smutty and tipsy songs contrast with Ariel's delicate airs.

44. scurvy fever contracted by sailors due to lack of the right vitamins, here used simply as 'rotten'.

44. at a man's funeral i.e. his own, just referred to in *die ashore,* or possibly Trinculo's, presumed drowned. Stephano is maudlin in his drunkenness, perhaps, with his only consolation for loneliness and sad thougths lying in his bottle.

46. swabber scrubber of the decks. The irony of Stephano's including himself in the list of genuine sailors, *master, boatswain,* etc., is that he is a land-lubber, on his first voyage, perhaps, to accompany Alonso to Tunis for the wedding.

48. Mall Maud.

48. Meg Margaret.

50. tang sting (i.e. a sharp tongue).

52. * She ... pitch i.e. she didn't like the smell of a ship, or of those from a ship. (Presumably *Mall* etc., are whores, perhaps those who are allowed aboard before the ship sails; and Kate, who may be one too but dislike sea-men, will only associate with a tailor, not a sailor, someone she can keep ashore.)

53. * Yet ... itch i.e. might be familiar or intimate with her. (*Tailor, scratch,* and *itch* probably all have sexual connotations.)

56. * Do not ... me Trinculo, trembling with fear that Stephano's voice (which he presumably recognizes) is that of a ghost (see line 86), is thought by Caliban to be a spirit preparing to torment him.

57. What's the matter? what's this?

57–8. * Do you ... of Ind? are you (devils, spirits) trying to deceive me by appearing as savages and Indians?

60. four legs Caliban's two legs point from under his gaberdine in one direction and Trinculo's in the other.

60–1. * As proper ... ground as excellent a man as ever walked on four legs (Stephano changes the proverbial 'two' to 'four' to match the Caliban-Trinculo monster he is looking at) cannot make this fellow (i.e. Caliban-Trinculo) retreat.

66. ague fever (because both Caliban and Trinculo are shaking with fear).

66–7. should he learn could he have learnt.

[Enter STEPHANO singing; a bottle in his hand]

Stephano

        I shall no more to sea, to sea,
        Here shall I die ashore –

This is a very scurvy tune to sing at a man's
funeral; well, here's my comfort.   45

[Drinks]

    The master, the swabber, the boatswain, and I,
    The gunner, and his mate,
    Lov'd Mall, Meg, and Marian, and Margery,
    But none of us car'd for Kate;
    For she had a tongue with a tang,   50
    Would cry to a sailor 'Go hang!'
    She lov'd not the savour of tar nor of pitch,
    Yet a tailor might scratch her where'er she did itch.
    Then to sea, boys, and let her go hang!

This is a scurvy tune too; but here's my comfort.   55

[Drinks]

Caliban

Do not torment me. O!

Stephano

What's the matter? Have we devils here? Do you
put tricks upon 's with savages and men of Ind? Ha!
I have not scap'd drowning to be afeard now of
your four legs; for it hath been said: As proper a   60
man as ever went on four legs cannot make him
give ground; and it shall be said so again, while
Stephano breathes at nostrils.

Caliban

The spirit torments me. O!

Stephano

This is some monster of the isle with four legs, who   65
hath got, as I take it, an ague. Where the devil should
he learn our language? I will give him some relief, if

68. recover revive. (Stephano's immediate reaction to this 'islander' is to help him only so that he can then exploit him, and in this attitude he resembles many of the explorers and colonists of the time.)

69. a present for a suitable present for.

69. neat's leather cowhide (shoes).

73. fit paroxysm of lunacy.

73. after the wisest very sensibly, very coherently.

76–7. * **I will ... for him** i.e. I shall expect a high price for him.

82. * **language ... cat** proverbially, liquor could make a cat speak. Prospero has already given Caliban language, and all that liquor is going to do is to make him a *howling monster* (line 174). By *give language* Stephano means 'loosen your tongue'. (The number of proverbs spoken in this scene may indicate the lower-class characters, who rely on proverbs to reconcile themselves to life's hardships. The use of repetitive phrases by Stephano may be a further indication of his limited intellect and rank, e.g. *scurvy tune, if I can recover him, and keep him tame, and that soundly, open your mouth.*)

84. * **you ... friend** you seem unable to understand that I'm your friend.

84. chaps jaws.

87. O, defend me! Trinculo invokes the aid of good angels to keep off devils.

88. delicate cleverly constructed, ingeniously formed.

89–90. * **forward ... backward** his voice in front pays compliments and his voice behind is derogatory and uncomplimentary. (There seem to be two ideas at work in what Stephano is saying: (a) he is calling the monster literally and metaphorically 'two-faced', (b) he is echoing Trinculo's *let loose*, line 34, in *backward voice ... foul,* which in turn prepares for the reference to *vent*, line 104.)

92. Come – Amen! come on, drink up whoa! that's enough!

it be but for that. If I can recover him, and keep him
tame, and get to Naples with him, he's a present for
any emperor that ever trod on neat's leather.   70

Caliban

Do not torment me, prithee; I'll bring my wood
home faster.

Stephano

He's in his fit now, and does not talk after the
wisest. He shall taste of my bottle; if he have never
drunk wine afore, it will go near to remove his fit. If   75
I can recover him, and keep him tame, I will not
take too much for him; he shall pay for him that
hath him, and that soundly.

Caliban

Thou dost me yet but little hurt; thou wilt anon, I
know it by thy trembling; now Prosper works upon   80
thee.

Stephano

Come on your ways; open your mouth; here is that
which will give language to you, cat. Open your
mouth; this will shake your shaking, I can tell you,
and that soundly; you cannot tell who's your friend.
Open your chaps again.   85

Trinculo

I should know that voice; it should be – but he is
drown'd; and these are devils. O, defend me!

Stephano

Four legs and two voices; a most delicate monster!
His forward voice, now, is to speak well of his
friend; his backward voice is to utter foul speeches   90
and to detract. If all the wine in my bottle will
recover him, I will help his ague. Come – Amen! I
will pour some in thy other mouth.

Trinculo

Stephano!

Stephano

Doth thy other mouth call me? Mercy, mercy! This   95

107

96–7. * I … spoon another proverb, i.e. that anyone supping with the Devil has need of a long spoon.

98–100. * Stephano … Trinculo Shakespeare fixes their names in the audience's minds by repetition: each name is used six times in this short dialogue.

98. touch me i.e. to show that he is Stephano and not a spirit. (Compare Prospero's embracing Alonso, Act V, Scene i, lines 108–9.)

99. be not afeard i.e. that I am a devil.

102. Trinculo's legs perhaps recognizable by the parti-coloured hose of a jester, or because *lesser*, thinner than Caliban's muscular and possibly misshapen legs.

102. very truly.

104. siege excrement. *Siege* primarily meant 'seat', and 'stool' is still used to refer to faeces. Trinculo has appeared from Caliban's 'behind'.

104. mooncalf i.e. the Moon's astrological influence has caused Caliban to be deformed before birth and has produced an abortive, misshapen monster.

104. vent emit, excrete.

106–7. * I hope … drowned i.e. that he (Trinculo) is not talking to the ghost of a drowned Stpehano.

109–10. two Neopolitans scap'd another use of dramatic irony (in that the audience knows of other Neopolitans who have escaped drowning).

111. turn me about i.e. perhaps Trinculo in his excitement is dancing round and round with him.

111. constant settled.

113. * these … sprites 'these are certainly fine beings if they are not spirits.' (Perhaps Caliban suspects that they must be spirits, to be so fine.)

117. * Swear … bottle i.e. Stephano is blasphemously using the bottle as a Bible (compare *kiss the book*, i.e. the bottle, in line 127). The wine, far from being *celestial liquor* which they can drink as gods, reduces them to beasts.

118–19. heav'd overboard either to lighten the ship in case it was running into shallow water or as something buoyant to cling to (as Stephano does) when they abandon ship.

is a devil, and no monster; I will leave him; I have
no long spoon.

Trinculo

Stephano! If thou beest Stephano, touch me, and
speak to me; for I am Trinculo – be not afeard – thy
good friend Trinculo. 100

Stephano

If thou beest Trinculo, come forth; I'll pull thee by
the lesser legs; if any be Trinculo's legs, these are
they. Thou art very Trinculo indeed! How cam'st
thou to be the siege of this moon-calf? Can he vent
Trinculos?

Trinculo

I took him to be kill'd with a thunderstroke. But art 105
thou not drown'd, Stephano? I hope now thou are
not drown'd. Is the storm overblown? I hid me
under the dead moon-calf's gaberdine for fear of
the storm. And art thou living, Stephano? O
Stephano, two Neapolitans scap'd! 110

Stephano

Prithee, do not turn me about; my stomach is not
constant.

Caliban [Aside]

These be fine things, an if they be not sprites.
That's a brave god, and bears celestial liquor.
I will kneel to him. 115

Stephano

How didst thou scape? How cam'st thou hither?
Swear by this bottle how thou cam'st hither – I
escap'd upon a butt of sack, which the sailors
heaved o'erboard – by this bottle, which I made of
the bark of a tree, with mine own hands, since I was 120
cast ashore.

Caliban

I'll swear upon that bottle to be thy true subject, for
the liquor is not earthly.

Stephano

Here; swear then how thou escap'dst.

128. like a goose the meaning is obscure. Possibly (a) he is (being a Jester or Court Fool) a 'giddy goose', or mad, (b) long-necked like the goose rather than short-necked like the duck, an allusion to his taking a long drink from the bottle, (c) lecherous ('goose' being associated with venereal disease in some of Shakespeare's plays).

134. Out o' th' moon Stephano, as many travellers were doing at that time, plays upon the simple credulity of the natives in primitive countries: he is delighted that Caliban should think him a god.

135. when time was once upon a time.

136. adore thee worship you (perhaps suitably, as a *mooncalf*).

137. * thee ... bush the patterns on the moon's surface portrayed the Man, who, with his dog, had been exiled to the Moon (according to popular legend) for gathering brushwood on a Sunday. His *bush* was his bundle of brushwood.

138–9. * furnish ... contents i.e. replenish it presently with more wine.

140. shallow ignorant, credulous.

140. * By ... light upon my soul.

141. weak foolish.

142. Well drawn that was a good swig (lit. 'draught').

144. * every ... inch Caliban possessed local knowledge of the island, and unless he showed the new settlers (which is what Stephano and Trinculo represent) the fertile parts they would soon starve.

146–7. * perfidious ... asleep (a) the treacherous behaviour of initially friendly natives was often reported by colonists in the New World, (b) in Act III, Scene ii, line 58, Caliban proposes to kill Prospero in his sleep.

Trinculo

Swum ashore, man, like a duck; I can swim like a   125
duck, I'll be sworn.

Stephano [Passing the bottle]

Here, kiss the book. Though thou canst swim like a
duck, thou art made like a goose.

Trinculo

O Stephano, hast any more of this?

Stephano

The whole butt, man; my cellar is in a rock by th'   130
seaside, where my wine is hid. How now, moon-
calf! How does thine ague?

Caliban

Hast thou not dropp'd from heaven?

Stephano

Out o' th' moon, I do assure thee; I was the Man i'
th' Moon, when time was.   135

Caliban

I have seen thee in her, and I do adore thee. My
mistress show'd me thee, and thy dog and thy bush.

Stephano

Come, swear to that; kiss the book. I will furnish it
anon with new contents. Swear.

[CALIBAN drinks]

Trinculo

By this good light, this is a very shallow monster! I   140
afeard of him! A very weak monster! The Man i' th'
Moon! A most poor credulous monster! Well
drawn, monster, in good sooth!

Caliban

I'll show thee every fertile inch o' th' island; and I
will kiss thy foot. I prithee be my god.   145

Trinculo

By this light, a most perfidious and drunken
monster! When 's god's asleep he'll rob his bottle.

150. puppy-headed stupid.
152–4. * beat him ... in drink the cowardly Trinculo, resenting Caliban's doglike devotion to Stephano, says that he would like to beat the kneeling Caliban. Perhaps Caliban turns on him and is only prevented from attacking him by Stephano's peremptory *Come, kiss.* Trinculo then saves his face by saying that he would not take unfair advantage of Caliban anyway, i.e. beat him when he's drunk.

156–60. * thee ... thou the repetition of *thee* in these lines shows Caliban transferring his allegiance from Prospero (*the tyrant*) to Stephano (*wondrous man*), but may also underline his antagonism towards Trinculo, which is used by Ariel (in Act III, Scene ii, lines 40–80).

160. wondrous man Caliban's admiration of Stephano can be contrasted with Ferdinand's of Miranda (Act I, Scene ii, line 427), Caliban's on the physical plane and produced by the intoxicating effects of wine, Ferdinand's on the spiritual and evoked by beauty.

163. crabs crab-apples.
164. pignuts earth-nuts.

166. marmoset small edible monkey.
167. filberts hazelnuts.
168. scamels the meaning is uncertain, but possible means 'god-wit', a curlew-like marsh bird; also possibly a 'sea-mell' or seamew.

171. we will inherit I, as king, will take possession (as next in succession after Alonso, etc.).
171. bear my bottle i.e. as royal cupbearer. Caliban's adulation of Stephano, and Stephano's drunkenness, make the royal butler behave condescendingly towards his equal, or near-equal, the royal jester, who now has the menial task of carrying the royal cup.
171. Fellow Trinculo to address a servant as 'fellow' if you were his superior was acceptable, but to address an equal as 'fellow' was a gross insult. Stephano is drunk with power as well as wine.

Caliban
I'll kiss thy foot; I'll swear myself thy subject.
Stephano
Come on, then; down, and swear.
Trinculo
I shall laugh myself to death at this puppy-headed   150
monster. A most scurvy monster! I could find in my
heart to beat him –
Stephano
Come, kiss.
Trinculo
But that the poor monster's in drink. An
abominable monster!   155
Caliban
I'll show thee the best springs; I'll pluck thee berries;
I'll fish for thee, and get thee wood enough.
A plague upon the tyrant that I serve!
I'll bear him no more sticks, but follow thee,
Thou wondrous man.   160
Trinculo
A most ridiculous monster, to make a wonder of a
poor drunkard!
Caliban
I prithee let me bring thee where crabs grow;
And I with my long nails will dig thee pig-nuts;
Show thee a jay's nest, and instruct thee how   165
To snare the nimble marmoset; I'll bring thee
To clust'ring filberts, and sometimes I'll get thee
Young scamels from the rock. Wilt thou go with me?
Stephano
I prithee now, lead the way without any more talking.
Trinculo, the King and all our company else being   170
drown'd, we will inherit here. Here, bear my bottle.
Fellow Trinculo, we'll fill him by and by again.
Caliban [Sings drunkenly]
          Farewell, master; farewell, farewell!

175. * **No more ... fish** natives of the New World used to help the early colonists by building dams so that fish could be got more easily, thus providing food without which they would often have starved.

176. firing firewood.

177. at requiring on demand.

178. trenchering wooden plates cleaned of food by *scraping*.

179. Ca-Caliban possibly a drunken 'hiccup'.

181. Freedom Caliban is in fact even less free than before, the servant of a servant, and slave to a bottle.

181. high-day! holiday! (perhaps granted to celebrate the accession of King Stephano?).

183. Lead the way The tipsy trio make a procession, Caliban leading, and Trinculo following Stephano. There is an ironic comment in this upon the end of the previous scene, when Alonso says *lead away* and the royal party proceeds on its way in search of Ferdinand.

By the end of Act II the initial development of each of the three situations is complete and the principal characters of the play have displayed their personalities in response to them. Each group is being (or, in the case of Ferdinand and Miranda, has already been) drawn towards Prospero's cell, partly by Ariel's music and partly by their own motivation.

Trinculo

A howling monster; a drunken monster!

Caliban

No more dams I'll make for fish;   175

Nor fetch in firing

At requiring,

Nor scrape trenchering, nor wash dish.

'Ban 'Ban, Ca – Caliban,

Has a new master – Get a new man.   180

Freedom, high-day! high-day, freedom! freedom,
high-day, freedom!

Stephano

O brave monster! Lead the way.

[Exeunt]

THE TEMPEST

ACT III

Scene I

This scene stands at mid-point in the play and provides its climax or turning-point, when Ferdinand and Miranda declare their love for one another; from this point there is no going back, Prospero's plans can now go forward to the eventual marriage of the lovers and forgiveness of those in the Alonso and Caliban groups. This declaration of love between the two young people makes possible the healing of the wounds of the older generation, and is the central moment of the drama.

Stage Direction. **bearing a log** the contrast between Ferdinand and Caliban (who has just said in his song that he will not *fetch in firing At requiring*) is vividly pointed. Perhaps the log is large enough to be used as a seat for Ferdinand's opening speech.

1–2. * There … sets off some forms of recreation can be quite tough, and the pleasure they provide makes up for the effort they demand.

2. baseness drudgery, servant's work.

3. nobly undergone accepted because they lead (i.e. the menial tasks) to noble results.

3. most perhaps 'the majority of poor' but possibly 'very' (i.e. 'some very lowly occupations').

4. mean task menial job, servile occupation.

5. * as … odious as oppressive as it is hateful.

5. but except for the fact that.

6. * mistress … serve Ferdinand uses the terms of the medieval courtly lover, over whom his lady-love was in complete command; her lightest wish it was his duty to perform without grudge or grumbling.

6. quickens revives me, raises my spirits (literally 'raises me from the dead').

8. crabbed sour, hard, 'difficult' (in contrast to the *gentle* Miranda, sweet, kind, and compassionate).

11. * Upon … injunction under threat of severe punishment.

11–12. * sweet … Weeps … sees the very sound of Miranda's voice is in these alliterations and assonances.

12–13. * such … executor such a menial task never had anyone as noble to perform it.

13. I forget i.e. I must get on with the job. Rested, he probably stands up to resume his labours.

15. * Most … do it i.e. I am most busily engaged (in thinking of Miranda) when I am least busily engaged (in doing my job).

Stage Direction. **at a distance** perhaps just outside his cell. On the raised rear level of the stage at an indoor performance, the position of the godlike father-figure of Prospero would be impressive, involved yet detached; particularly so when he invokes the heavens to bless the couple (lines 75–6).

17. enjoin'd sworn, obliged by oath.

18–19. * when … weep when this log is burning it will ooze with resin (i.e. nature will sympathize with you, as I do, by weeping). Compare Act I, Scene ii, line 150, where the winds are described as sighing in sympathy.

ACT THREE

SCENE I. Before Prospero's cell.

[Enter FERDINAND, bearing a log]

Ferdinand
There be some sports are painful, and their labour
Delight in them sets off; some kinds of baseness
Are nobly undergone, and most poor matters
Point to rich ends. This my mean task
Would be as heavy to me as odious, but   5
The mistress which I serve quickens what's dead,
And makes my labours pleasures. O, she is
Ten times more gentle than her father's crabbed;
And he's compos'd of harshness. I must remove
Some thousands of these logs, and pile them up,   10
Upon a sore injunction; my sweet mistress
Weeps when she sees me work, and says such
     baseness
Had never like executor. I forget;
But these sweet thoughts do even refresh my
     labours,
Most busy, least when I do it.

[Enter MIRANDA; and PROSPERO at a distance, unseen]

Miranda   Alas, now; pray you,   15
Work not so hard; I would the lightning had
Burnt up those logs that you are enjoin'd to pile.
Pray, set it down and rest you; when this burns,
'Twill weep for having wearied you. My father

117

21. safe safely out of the way. Another obvious dramatic irony, Prospero standing *unseen* behind them.

22. * The sun ... set (a) together with Miranda's *these three hours*, this is a reminder of time passing, (b) the folk-tale situation of a young suitor given an almost impossible task to complete (as a test of his manhood) before sundown in order to win a fair princess is also perhaps suggested, (compare folk-tales in which the hero has to cut down a wood to clear the ground for ploughing and then reap the harvest, the three actions to be completed by him on a single day).

24. the while for the time being. Rhyming seems to occur in *while ... pile, crack ... back, do it ... to it*; and the formality and artificiality given by rhyme are supported by the balanced alternation of identically-organized short speeches from Ferdinand and Miranda, i.e. *O most dear ... strive to do* is mirrored by *If you'll ... the pile*, and *No, precious ... sit lazy by* by *It would ... it is against*. Something rather like an operatic duet is suggested by the precise to-and-fro of the dialogue, and is perhaps deliberately used by Shakespeare to symbolize and express a perfect pairing.

26. crack strain (pull a muscle).

28. become me be as fitting for me.

30. much more ease much more readily.

31–2. * Poor ... shows it poor creature, you are strongly affected by love! This 'attack' shows that clearly. (Miranda is described as having caught the 'plague' of love.) Perhaps Ferdinand, if he put the log back on his shoulders at line 14, puts it down again during lines 31–2.

33–4. * 'tis ... night Ferdinand speaks figuratively, not literally (they have only known each other for an hour or two of daylight), i.e. she revives him as dawn does by being with him during his 'dead' time (night) of log-lugging.

35. in my prayers i.e. a suitable setting for the name of *goddess*, perhaps like a rich jewel.

37. broke your hest disobeyed your command.

37. Admir'd Miranda the name Miranda means 'worthy to be wondered at' or 'worthy of admiration'.

39. * What's ... world e.g. the richest jewel, the most precious object.

40. * ey'd ... regard looked at appreciatively, given the 'glad eye'.

41–2. * Th' harmony ... ear my susceptible ear has been captivated by the sweet music of their voices. The senses of sight and hearing, so often referred to in the play, are again present in lines 40–2.

42. several separate, different.

43–5. * never ow'd never any one of them, for, however perfect, she always had some deficiency which conflicted with the finest quality she possessed.

46. put it to the foil either (a) the *defect* cancelled out the *grace*, or (b) the *defect* heightened the lustre of the *grace*. In (a) *foil* is an image from wrestling, *foil* meaning a throw (as in the modern sense of 'foiling an attempt'), and in (b) *foil* is an image from the dark background (often black velvet) used by jewellers to show off a jewel. *Quarrel* in line 45 may also suggest *foil*: sword.

Is hard at study; pray, now, rest yourself;   20
  He's safe for these three hours.
Ferdinand   O most dear mistress,
  The sun will set before I shall discharge
  What I must strive to do.
Miranda   If you'll sit down,
  I'll bear your logs the while; pray give me that;
  I'll carry it to the pile.
Ferdinand   No, precious creature;   25
  I had rather crack my sinews, break my back,
  Than you should such dishonour undergo,
  While I sit lazy by.
Miranda   It would become me
  As well as it does you; and I should do it   30
  With much more ease; for my good will is to it,
  And yours it is against.
Prospero [Aside]   Poor worm, thou art infected!
  This visitation shows it.

Miranda   You look wearily.

Ferdinand
  No, noble mistress; 'tis fresh morning with me
  When you are by at night. I do beseech you,
  Chiefly that I might set it in my prayers,   35
  What is your name?
Miranda   Miranda – O my father,
  I have broke your hest to say so!
Ferdinand   Admir'd Miranda!
  Indeed the top of admiration; worth
  What's dearest to the world! Full many a lady
  I have ey'd with best regard; and many a time   40
  Th' harmony of their tongues hath into bondage
  Brought my too diligent ear; for several virtues
  Have I lik'd several women, never any
  With so full soul, but some defect in her
  Did quarrel with the noblest grace she ow'd,   45
  And put it to the foil; but you, O you,

47. peerless unrivalled.

48. every creature's best the best quality of every created being.

37–48. * Ferdinand's speech contains a considerable number of repetitions (*Admir'd* and *Miranda, many … many, several … several, you, O you, created … creature*) which perhaps add to the lyrical and 'operatic' effect. It is as if Ferdinand is rejoicing at the gift of Miranda's name, which is symbolic of her giving herself to him (and in marriage she will give up her name to him, in a sense), and she then replies to him in a speech of precisely the same length (i.e. a half-line, ten lines, a half-line).

50. glass mirror.

51. * **More … you** i.e. Caliban does not count as a man. Miranda, by juxtaposing Caliban and Ferdinand, implies the contrast between them.

52. features appearance (not simply faces), what people look like.

52. abroad in the world generally.

53. I am skilless of I have no idea.

54. * **jewel … dower** Miranda has nothing (which is, in fact, everything) to offer this prince (now, apparently, a king) in the way of dowry to give him when they are married but the most precious quality she can possess, her 'modesty'. (The jewel image is repeated.)

56–7. * **Nor … like of** nor can my imagination create any being other than you whom I would want.

58. precepts instructions, (presumably not to talk too much to Ferdinand, and thereby seem 'forward' or immodest).

59. condition rank.

61. I would not so! Ferdinand, unlike Antonio and Sebastian, has no ambition to be King if it means the d·ath of Alonso.

62–3. * **suffer … mouth** allow a blow-fly to foul my lips (by laying its eggs on my lips).

63. my soul i.e. my love for you is not merely physical, or of the mind, but from my very spirit.

65. * **fly … service** i.e. like a bird, or an arrow, or perhaps Ariel, directly, straight, speedily, in a flash.

68. this sound i.e. my words.

69. what I profess my declaration of love.

69. kind event happy result, outcome.

70–1. * **If hollowly … mischief** if I speak insincerely, turn the best that the future has in store for me into the worst.

72. * **Beyond … world** i.e. beyond anything you can imagine.

73. love, prize, honour Ferdinand makes his unequivocal declaration of love. This line can perhaps be considered the exact climax of the play, the turning-point towards which the central action has been rising. From this point the falling action begins to move towards its inevitable outcome, the uniting of the lovers in marriage.

74. encounter meeting.

75–6. * **Heavens … between 'em** the image combines the astrological shedding of influence by the planetary gods (*rain grace*) with that of fertility (*breeds*). The Masque in Act IV, Scene i repeats the same ideas. Miranda's weeping with joy is also a fruitful rain, expressing and nourishing love.

75–6. that which breeds i.e. that which is developing.

So perfect and so peerless, are created
Of every creature's best!

Miranda   I do not know
One of my sex; no woman's face remember,
Save, from my glass, mine own; nor have I seen   50
More that I may call men than you, good friend,
And my dear father. How features are abroad,
I am skilless of; but, by my modesty,
The jewel in my dower, I would not wish
Any companion in the world but you;   55
Nor can imagination form a shape,
Besides yourself, to like of. But I prattle
Something too wildly, and my father's precepts
I therein do forget.

Ferdinand   I am, in my condition,
A prince, Miranda; I do think, a king –   60
I would not so! – and would no more endure
This wooden slavery than to suffer
The flesh-fly blow my mouth. Hear my soul speak:
The very instant that I saw you, did
My heart fly to your service; there resides   65
To make me slave to it; and for your sake
Am I this patient log-man.

Miranda   Do you love me?

Ferdinand
O heaven, O earth, bear witness to this sound,
And crown what I profess with kind event,
If I speak true! If hollowly, invert   70
What best is boded me to mischief! I,
Beyond all limit of what else i' th' world,
Do love, prize, honour you.

Miranda   I am a fool
To weep at what I am glad of.

Prospero [Aside]   Fair encounter
Of two most rare affections! Heavens rain grace   75
On that which breeds between 'em!

Ferdinand   Wherefore weep you?

77–9. * **that dare ... to want** i.e. Miranda does not dare to offer him the love she wants to give him, and feels even less worthy to accept his love, without which she will die.

77–9. to want through lack (of it).

80–1. * **And all ... it shows** i.e. the more she tries to hide the fact that she loves him, the more obvious it becomes that she does. (The image of *bigger bulk* suggests pregnancy, following *breeds* in line 76, which is the result of love.)

82. prompt me inspire me.

84. maid (a) unmarried, (b) maidservant. (Compare Act I, Scene ii, lines 428–9.)

84. fellow mate, equal (as wife) as a companion, consort, spouse.

85. servant both Ferdinand and Miranda have shown themselves to be ideal lovers in their desire to serve each other.

87. thus humble Perhaps Ferdinand is kneeling to her. Humility being the chief of the cardinal virtues, as the antithesis of pride (deadliest of the deadly sins), so in the 'religion of love', the chivalrous code of conduct followed by medieval knights towards their ladies, the young knight knelt to his lady in humble service to his 'saint'.

89. * **As bondage ... freedom** as the bondman or bondslave is to be free. (Ferdinand uses an *apparently* incongruous simile: he has just bound himself to Miranda's service, and yet uses a simile which describes the joy of the servant who has just been released from his obligation to his master. In fact the simile is apt, because Ferdinand paradoxically *wants* to be Miranda's servant: her 'service is perfect freedom'.)

91. thousand thousand Ferdinand wishes Miranda a million (i.e. unlimited) 'fare-thee-wells'.

Stage Direction. **severally** in opposite directions, Ferdinand having to carry off the log he entered with.

92–3. * **So glad ... withal** I cannot be as overjoyed at this (revelation of love) as they are, because it has taken them, but not me, by surprise.

94. book perhaps to prepare for the impressive displays of magical power in the Banquet scene (Act III, Scene iii) and the Masque (Act IV, Scene i), particularly the latter (see note below).

95–6. * **perform ... appertaining** carry out a great deal in connection with this love-match (i.e. the Masque to celebrate a *contract of true love*, Act IV, Scene i, line 84).

95–6. perform hints at the Masque, a performance of which Prospero is to put on, to stage, rather than perform in, take a part, himself.

The lyrical dignity of this short scene is heightened by its obvious contrast with the coarse scenes in prose which precede and follow it. The drunken behaviour and crude songs of Act II, Scene ii, and the brutish violence of Act III, scene ii act as dark 'foils' (to use Shakespeare's own metaphor) between which Act III, scene i shines, in its balanced and harmonious language, like a bright jewel.

Miranda

  At mine unworthiness, that dare not offer
  What I desire to give, and much less take
  What I shall die to want. But this is trifling;
  And all the more it seeks to hide itself,   80
  The bigger bulk it shows. Hence, bashful cunning!
  And prompt me plain and holy innocence!
  I am your wife, if you will marry me;
  If not, I'll die your maid. To be your fellow
  You may deny me; but I'll be your servant,   85
  Whether you will or no.

Ferdinand   My mistress, dearest;
  And I thus humble ever.

Miranda   My husband, then?

Ferdinand

  Ay, with a heart as willing
  As bondage e'er of freedom. Here's my hand.

Miranda

  And mine, with my heart in't. And now farewell   90
  Till half an hour hence.

Ferdinand   A thousand thousand!

    [Exeunt FERDINAND and MIRANDA severally]

Prospero

  So glad of this as they I cannot be,
  Who are surpris'd withal; but my rejoicing
  At nothing can be more. I'll to my book;
  For yet ere supper time must I perform   95
  Much business appertaining.

               [Exit]

ACT III SCENE II

The main purpose of this scene is to take the degeneration of the comic trio, which began in Act II, scene ii, to its next stage, from drunkenness to plans for murder. In the process their relationships with one another deteriorate: Stephano becomes a mere tyrant (not at all the king that he would like to imagine he is), Trinculo an envious coward, and Caliban more and more incredulous at the lack of courage and single-mindedness of his heroes. They are no real threat to Prospero, and Ariel makes fools of them. By letting the audience laugh, Shakespeare provides another break, after the delicate intensity of the scene between the two lovers, and before returning to the Alonso situation at its climax.

1. Tell not me perhaps Trinculo has been suggesting that Stephano ought to ration the sack (white wine) which won't last long at this rate of consumption. In his drunken vanity, Stephano insists on being toasted by Caliban.

2. bear up and board 'em drink up. The image is from sea-warfare (compare 'up Guards and at 'em'). Perhaps Stephano's *Coragio* (Act V, Scene i, line 257) has the same force, 'be of good courage', before the hand-to-hand fighting.

4. folly (a) freak i.e. because he is a monster suitable for exhibition at a fair, (b) foolishness produced by being on the island.

6. be brain'd like us have brains like ours (i.e. fuddled by liquor: compare Act V, Scene I, lines 59–60 where Alonso and his courtiers' brains are *useless, boil'd* within their skulls).

8. * set ... head unseeing, glazed.

10. tail bottom (compare the coarse jokes of Act II, Scene ii).

11. man-monster manservant-monster.

12–14. * For ... off and on Stephano's drunken boastfulness is shown here.

12–14. five and thirty leagues would be 105 miles.

12–14. recover reach.

15. standard standard-bearer, ensign.

16. no standard i.e. Caliban is horizontal (lying on the ground) rather than vertical (standing upright).

17. run run away (i.e. from the enemy in battle. The flag or standard had to be kept flying as a rallying point and to show your troops that you were still fighting.)

18. go walk (because they are too drunk to).

18. lie (a) tell lies, (b) lie down. Trinculo may again be using words in a coarse secondary sense (e.g. *run:* make water, *lie:* excrete).

SCENE II. Another part of the island.

[Enter CALIBAN, STEPHANO and TRINCULO]

Stephano

Tell not me – when the butt is out we will drink
water, not a drop before; therefore bear up, and
board 'em. Servant-monster, drink to me.

Trinculo

Servant-monster! The folly of this island! They say
there's but five upon this isle: we are three of them;   5
if th' other two be brain'd like us, the state totters.

Stephano

Drink, servant-monster, when I bid thee; thy eyes
are almost set in thy head.

Trinculo

Where should they be set else? He were a brave
monster indeed, if they were set in his tail.   10

Stephano

My man-monster hath drown'd his tongue in sack.
For my part, the sea cannot drown me; I swam, ere
I could recover the shore, five and thirty leagues, off
and on. By this light, thou shalt be my lieutenant,
monster, or my standard.   15

Trinculo

Your lieutenant, if you list; he's no standard.

Stephano

We'll not run, Monsieur Monster.

Trinculo

Nor go neither; but you'll lie like dogs, and yet say
nothing neither.

Stephano

Moon-calf, speak once in thy life, if thou beest a   20
good moon-calf.

Caliban

How does thy honour? Let me lick thy shoe.
I'll not serve him; he is not valiant.

24. in case ready to, in the right condition to.
24. justle jostle, shove around (i.e. in order to provoke). A modern equivalent might be 'to go and knock a policeman's helmet off'.
25. debosh'd debauched, depraved.
26. * coward ... sack i.e. drunk so much wine to give him 'Dutch courage', false courage produced by intoxication.

31. natural idiot, simpleton, half-wit. (Ironically, Caliban is 'unnatural', an abortion in nature.)

34. prove turn out to be.
34. the next tree i.e. will be his gallows.

36–7. * I thank ... thee Shakespeare's contempt of fawning is seen in this parody of court behaviour, and is a reminder of Act I, Scene ii, line 79.

38. Marry, will I indeed I will. (*Marry* is a corrupt form of 'By the Virgin Mary'.)
38. I will stand as Alonso's butler, Stephano perhaps remembers court protocol. With Trinculo and Stephano swaying tipsily, and Caliban crouching before them, the scene would make an ironic comment on European court life, and a sad one on the 'fatal impact' made by the explorers of the New World upon the natives they dominate.

Stage Direction. **Enter Ariel** presumably placing himself behind or near to Trinculo.

43. jesting monkey i.e. Trinculo is a meddling (monkey) jester (court fool).
47. supplant remove, knock out. (*supplant* is used in Act II, Scene i, line 267 and Act III, Scene iii, line 70 in reference to Prospero's usurpation. This may be pure coincidence, but could be an example of the way in which what is important in the main situations of the play is trivialized in the 'comic trio' scenes, often with ironic effect.)

Trinculo

Thou liest, most ignorant monster: I am in case to
justle a constable. Why, thou debosh'd fish, thou,   25
was there ever man a coward that hath drunk so
much sack as I to-day? Wilt thou tell a monstrous
lie, being but half a fish and half a monster?

Caliban

Lo, how he mocks me! Wilt thou let him, my lord?

Trinculo

'Lord' quoth he! That a monster should be such a   30
natural!

Caliban

Lo, lo again! Bite him to death, I prithee.

Stephano

Trinculo, keep a good tongue in your head; if you
prove a mutineer – the next tree! The poor monster's
my subject, and he shall not suffer indignity.   35

Caliban

I thank my noble lord. Wilt thou be pleas'd to
hearken once again to the suit I made to thee?

Stephano

Marry will I; kneel and repeat it; I will stand, and
so shall Trinculo.

[Enter ARIEL, invisible]

Caliban

As I told thee before, I am subject to a tyrant, a   40
sorcerer, that by his cunning hath cheated me of
the island.

Ariel

Thou liest.

Caliban

          Thou liest, thou jesting monkey, thou;
I would my valiant master would destroy thee.
I do not lie.   45

Stephano

Trinculo, if you trouble him any more in's tale, by
this hand, I will supplant some of your teeth.

49. Mum be silent ('Mum's the word').

53. this thing i.e. Trinculo (a mere monkey rather than a man).

56. compass'd achieved, encompassed.
57. party person.

58. yield him thee deliver him into your hands.
59. * knock ... head as Jael did to the sleeping Sisera (*Judges* IV.21). To kill a sleeping person was despicable cowardice (compare the plot to murder Alonso, and the murders of Duncan in *Macbeth* and old Hamlet in *Hamlet*).

61. pied ninny a reference to Trinculo's parti-coloured (*pied*) 'motley' to denote the jester. *ninny* is from 'innocent'.
61. scurvy patch 'moth-eaten fool'. (Scurvy produced a patchy skin condition, and patch could also refer to the jester's costume being in patches of colour.)

65. quick freshes flowing fresh-water streams (in contrast to (a) the sea-water (*brine*) and (b) to the *filthy-mantled pool* of Act IV, Scene i, line 182, which is where they are soon to find themselves).

68. stock-fish dried cod (which had been beaten before being boiled).

Trinculo
  Why, I said nothing.
Stephano
  Mum, then, and no more. Proceed.
Caliban
  I say, by sorcery he got this isle;   50
  From me he got it. If thy greatness will
  Revenge it on him – for I know thou dar'st,
  But this thing dare not –
Stephano
  That's most certain.
Caliban
  Thou shalt be lord of it, and I'll serve thee.   55
Stephano
  How now shall this be compass'd? Canst thou bring
      me to the party?
Caliban
  Yea, yea my lord; I'll yield him thee asleep,
  Where thou mayst knock a nail into his head.
Ariel
  Thou liest; thou canst not.   60
Caliban
  What a pied ninny's this! Thou scurvy patch!
  I do beseech thy greatness, give him blows,
  And take his bottle from him. When that's gone
  He shall drink nought but brine; for I'll not show
      him
  Where the quick freshes are.   65
Stephano
  Trinculo, run into no further danger; interrupt the
  monster one word further and, by this hand, I'll turn
  my mercy out o' doors, and make a stock-fish of thee.
Trinculo
  Why, what did I? I did nothing. I'll go farther off.
Stephano
  Didst thou not say he lied?   70
Ariel
  Thou liest.

72–3. * As you ... another time If you like being beaten, accuse me again to my face of lying.

74–5. * Out ... too are you out of your mind and deaf as well?

75–6. * This ... do this is what drink can do to a man.

75–6. murrain cattle-disease (suitable to plague a *mooncalf*).

76–7. * devil ... fingers i.e. may you lose your fingers (for beating me).

79–80. * Prithee ... off presumably said to Trinculo, though possibly to Caliban if Stephano can no longer stand his *fishlike smell* of body-odour close to him.

81. * after ... too although Caliban is not *afeard* of the strange noises on the island, he shows himself cowardly in telling Stephano how to kill Prospero rather than performing the murder himself.

84. there at that time, then.

85, 88, 91. books Caliban stresses the importance of Prospero's volumes of magic 'art'. His attitude is that of illiterate suspicion and perhaps symbolic of the prejudice of the uneducated against research and learning in general. It is significant that he only wishes to destroy the books, not to profit by studying them.

85. log this would no doubt give Caliban particular pleasure.

86. * paunch ... stake thrust a sharpened stake into his stomach. (*Brain* and *paunch*, normally nouns, have great vigour as verbs.)

87. wezand wind-pipe.

89. sot powerless fool.

92. brave utensils fine household objects (no doubt included, e.g. *trenchering* and *dish* among them, by Gonzalo as *necessaries* when Prospero and Miranda were put into the *carcass of a butt*).

92. for so he calls them Caliban's limited vocabulary is again suggested: he is simply quoting Prospero in using the word *utensil* (compare *nonpareil*, line 96).

93. * Which ... withal which he will display in his house when he has one.

94. * And that ... is and that which is most seriously to be considered is.

96. nonpareil matchless in beauty, unrivalled (see note to line 92).

97–8. * Sycorax ... she ... she ... Sycorax the inverted repetition of the words reinforces the contrast between pure ugliness (spiritual and physical) and pure beauty (spiritual and physical).

99. * great'st ... least i.e. Sycorax and Miranda are as widely separated as the two ends of any scale you choose. This sort of extreme comparison can be found elsewhere in the play, e.g. Act I, Scene ii, lines 481–2 and Act III, Scene i, lines 8–9, and contributes to making the characters 'ideal' rather than 'real', i.e. no one in real life is *all* good or *all* bad.

Stephano

Do I so? Take thou that. [Beats him] As you like
this, give me the lie another time.

Trinculo

I did not give the lie. Out o' your wits and hearing
too? A pox o' your bottle! This can sack and   75
drinking do. A murrain on your monster, and the
devil take your fingers!

Caliban

Ha, ha, ha!

Stephano

Now, forward with your tale. – Prithee stand further
off.   80

Caliban

Beat him enough; after a little time, I'll beat him
too.

Stephano

Stand farther. Come, proceed.

Caliban

Why, as I told thee, 'tis a custom with him
I' th' afternoon to sleep; there thou mayst brain him,
Having first seiz'd his books; or with a log   85
Batter his skull, or paunch him with a stake,
Or cut his wezand with thy knife. Remember
First to possess his books; for without them
He's but a sot, as I am, nor hath not
One spirit to command; they all do hate him   90
As rootedly as I. Burn but his books.
He has brave utensils – for so he calls them –
Which, when he has a house, he'll deck withal.
And that most deeply to consider is
The beauty of his daughter; he himself   95
Calls her a nonpareil. I never saw a woman
But only Sycorax my dam and she;
But she as far surpasseth Sycorax
As great'st does least.

Stephano   Is it so brave a lass?

100. become grace, adorn.
100. warrant assure you, guarantee.
101. brave brood fine offspring. (The attraction of Miranda so far as Caliban and Stephano are concerned is wholly sexual. Perhaps there is also a reference here to New World settlers needing to raise large families quickly to provide enough hands to raise enough crops to survive.)
104. viceroys Stephano thinks in terms of show (titles). They are not going to have any subjects to rule, anyway. (Here again there is a comment implied on Antonio and Sebastian who are ambitious for positions and power.)
105. plot plan, idea, scheme.

109. half-hour a reminder of the pressure of time: events are gathering to a head.

113. jocund gay, cheerful.
113. troll sing heartily, 'belt out'.
113. the catch the song (a part-song, with each singer in turn starting to sing, the first line as the singer before him finishes it, and so in successive lines).
114. while-ere a short while ago.
115. do reason do anything within reason.

117. * Flout ... scout sneer and jeer.

119. Thought is free proverbial.
    Stage Direction. **tabor and pipe** the actor playing Ariel was presumably trained in this difficult act of co-ordination, tapping the basic rhythm on the side drum (*tabor*) with one hand and playing a recorder (*pipe*) with the other.

Caliban

  Ay, lord; she will become thy bed, I warrant,   100

  And bring thee forth brave brood.

Stephano

  Monster, I will kill this man; his daughter and I will

  be King and Queen – save our Graces! – and

  Trinculo and thyself shall be viceroys. Dost thou

  like the plot, Trinculo?   105

Trinculo

  Excellent.

Stephano

  Give me thy hand; I am sorry I beat thee; but while

  thou liv'st, keep a good tongue in thy head.

Caliban

  Within this half hour will he be asleep.

  Wilt thou destroy him then?

Stephano   Ay, on mine honour.   110

Ariel

  This will I tell my master.

Caliban

  Thou mak'st me merry; I am full of pleasure.

  Let us be jocund; will you troll the catch

  You taught me but while-ere?

Stephano

  At thy request, monster, I will do reason, any   115

  reason. Come on, Trinculo, let us sing.

           [Sings]

      Flout 'em and scout 'em,

      And scout 'em and flout 'em;

        Thought is free.

Caliban

  That's not the tune.   120

    [ARIEL plays the tune on a tabor and pipe]

121–9. * What ... mercy on us! from boastful bawling of the song, Stephano and Trinculo are suddenly reduced to awed silence. Wonder (lines 121–3) turns to challenge (line 124), then to fear in Trinculo (line 126), and finally to an attempt at bravado by Stephano (line 127) which crumbles into panic. Caliban is astonished at the behaviour of his hero (line 129).

122–3. picture of Nobody a reference to a well-known broadsheet illustration of the time depicting a man with head, arms and legs but no body.

124–5. * If thou ... thou list if you are a man, show yourself to be one by appearing; if you are a devil, then take any form you wish.

131. noises musical sounds.

133. twangling stringed (a word formed by a combination of 'twanging' and 'jangling', perhaps).

134. hum like bees, or perhaps humming birds.

134. voices singing.

131–9. * In a speech of pathos and lyricism, Caliban is for a moment transformed from a purely animal being into a spiritual one. In so doing he symbolizes one of the central themes of the play, the power of the divine (as expressed in love and harmony) over the earthly. As in Ferdinand's speech (Act III, Scene i, lines 37–48), some of the lyricism is achieved by use of repetition (*sometimes ... sometime, sleep ... sleep, wak'd ... wak'd, dreaming ... dream*) and some by soft 's' and 'm' alliteration together with rhyming effects, *noises ... voices, some ... hum*.

141. music for nothing a characteristically mean attitude by Stephano ('something for nothing', like unearned titles) and typical perhaps of someone with no ear for music, (*That's not the tune*, says Caliban, who has an ear for music, in line 120).

142. * When ... destroyed the simple but strong singlemindedness of the savage contrasts with the easily distracted shallowness of the 'civilized' Stephano.

144. after i.e. pleasure before business (the bloody business).

Stephano

  What is this same?

Trinculo

  This is the tune of our catch, play'd by the picture
  of Nobody.

Stephano

  If thou beest a man, show thyself in thy likeness; if
  thou beest a devil, take't as thou list.   125

Trinculo

  O, forgive me my sins!

Stephano

  He that dies pays all debts. I defy thee. Mercy upon
  us!

Caliban

  Art thou afeard?

Stephano

  No, monster, not I.   130

Caliban

  Be not afeard. The isle is full of noises,
  Sounds, and sweet airs, that give delight, and hurt
      not.
  Sometimes a thousand twangling instruments
  Will hum about mine ears; and sometime voices,
  That, if I then had wak'd after long sleep,   135
  Will make me sleep again; and then, in dreaming,
  The clouds methought would open and show riches
  Ready to drop upon me, that, when I wak'd,
  I cried to dream again.

Stephano

  This will prove a brave kingdom to me, where I   140
  shall have my music for nothing.

Caliban

  When Prospero is destroy'd.

Stephano

  That shall be by and by; I remember the story.

Trinculo

  The sound is going away; let's follow it, and after
  do our work.   145

146. Lead, monster i.e. as standard-bearer and protector of his 'king'. (*Lead*: compare Act II, Scene i, line 319 and Act II, Scene ii, line 182.)

147. lays it on i.e. beats the drum with compelling urgency (and draws them like children following a fife-and-drum recruiting band).

148. Wilt come? perhaps said to Caliban, who might be heading for Prospero's cell while Ariel leads them away from it, but more likely to Stephano, who is looking around for *this taborer*.

148. I'll follow partly as a subordinate, but mainly for fear of being separated from Stephano and meeeting a 'devil', or being left alone with his enemy, Caliban.

As the trio leave the stage at the end of this scene, we can contrast their puzzled departure with their confident exit at the end of Act II, scene ii; and we can compare it with that of the royal party at the end of Act II, scene i, going with fear and wonder into the unknown. Both groups are now beginning to *suffer a sea change*.

SCENE III

When the clowns begin their painful journey to the stagnant pool, the royal group complete the next stage of their journey towards self-knowledge and reach the turning point of the play's action. Once they have heard the charge given by Ariel they are imprisoned by their guilty feelings and can be released at the end of the play only when redeemed by the lovers and pardoned by Prospero.

1. By'r lakin by our Ladykin (little lady, the Virgin Mary).

2–3. * Here's ... meanders Gonzalo compares the natural paths through the undergrowth with an artificial maze (e.g. at Hampton Court), in which there are straight paths (*forthrights*) and twisting ones (*meanders*).

5. attach'd seized (literally 'arrested'), overcome.

6. To th' dulling which deadens.

7–8. * Even ... flatterer this is the place where I will finally give up hope and keep it no longer to flatter me. (i.e. like a courtier trying to persuade me that Ferdinand is still alive). The image is (in *put off*) of the king doffing his royal robe: he can no longer delude himself that Ferdinand will one day wear it (i.e. succeed him).

10. frustrate vain, useless.

12–13. * Do not ... t'effect don't, because of one setback, give up the plan you were determined to carry out.

13. advantage favourable opportunity.

14. throughly thoroughly.

Stephano
　Lead, monster; we'll follow. I would I could see this
　taborer; he lays it on.
Trinculo
　Wilt come? I'll follow, Stephano.

[Exeunt]

SCENE III. Another part of the island.

[Enter ALONSO, SEBASTIAN, ANTONIO, GONZALO,
ADRIAN, FRANCISCO, and OTHERS]

Gonzalo
　By'r lakin, I can go no further, sir;
　My old bones ache. Here's a maze trod, indeed,
　Through forth-rights and meanders! By your
　　　　patience,
　I needs must rest me.
Alonso　　　　　　　Old lord, I cannot blame thee,
　Who am myself attach'd with weariness　　　　　　　5
　To th' dulling of my spirits; sit down and rest.
　Even here I will put off my hope, and keep it
　No longer for my flatterer; he is drown'd
　Whom thus we stray to find, and the sea mocks
　Our frustrate search on land. Well, let him go.　　　10
Antonio [Aside to SEBASTIAN]
　I am right glad that he's so out of hope.
　Do not, for one repulse, forgo the purpose
　That you resolv'd t' effect.
Sebastian [Aside to ANTONIO]
　　　　　　　　　　The next advantage
　Will we take throughly.
Antonio　[Aside to SEBASTIAN]
　　　　　　　　　　Let it be to-night;
　For, now they are oppress'd with travel, they　　　15
　Will not, nor cannot, use such vigilance

137

Stage Direction. **solemn** ceremonious, formal. **strange music** perhaps hautboys (oboes) to give a supernatural effect.

Stage Direction. **on the top** on the upper stage, perhaps, but more probably on the top stage or musicians' gallery above the upper stage to give the effect of a 'god' controlling this spectacular example of his art which he has conjured up.

20. **kind keepers** guardian angels.

21. **A living drollery** a puppet show with living, flesh-and-blood figures.

21. **Now I will believe** i.e. even the sceptical Sebastian (like Antonio: *I'll believe both*, line 24) is convinced.

22–3. * **unicorns ... phoenix** legendary, fabulous creatures, (a) the unicorn, a pure white horse with single horn, symbolized purity, and (b) the phoenix, a unique bird living in Arabia, which every five hundred years died by cremating itself and creating from its own ashes another unique phoenix, was a symbol of resurrection and hope. (It is perhaps ironical that Sebastian chooses two mythical creatures so appropriate to the central idea of the play.)

25. * **what ... credit** whatever else needs to be believed (i.e. is difficult to accept).

26. * **travellers ... lie** i.e. no travellers' tales, however far-fetched they might seem, were 'tall stories' (because what Antonio has witnessed is much less credible).

30. **certes** certainly.

31. **monstrous shape** strange, unnatural appearance.

32. **gentle-kind** the phrase combines the natural gentleness of unspoilt natives with what is desirable in European nobles.

33. **generation** breed, race.

34. **Honest** honourable.

36. **muse** wonder at.

As when they are fresh.
Sebastian [Aside to ANTONIO]
                    I say, to-night; no more.

[Solemn and strange music; and PROSPERO on the
top, invisible. Enter several strange SHAPES, bringing
in a banquet; and dance about it with gentle actions
of salutations; and inviting the KING, etc., to eat, they
                    depart]

Alonso
  What harmony is this? My good friends, hark!
Gonzalo
  Marvellous sweet music!
Alonso
  Give us kind keepers, heavens! What were these?   20
Sebastian
  A living drollery. Now I will believe
  That there are unicorns; that in Arabia
  There is one tree, the phoenix' throne, one phoenix
  At this hour reigning there.
Antonio
  I'll believe both;
  And what does else want credit, come to me,   25
  And I'll be sworn 'tis true; travellers ne'er did lie,
  Though fools at home condemn 'em.
Gonzalo   If in Naples
  I should report this now, would they believe me?
  If I should say, I saw such islanders,
  For certes these are people of the island,   30
  Who though they are of monstrous shape yet, note,
  Their manners are more gentle-kind than of
  Our human generation you shall find
  Many, nay, almost any.
Prospero [Aside]   Honest lord,
  Thou hast said well; for some of you there present   35
  Are worse than devils.
Alonso   I cannot too much muse

38. want lack.

39. dumb discourse i.e speaking in actions (as in the party game, 'dumb crambo').

39. Praise in departing a proverbial expression meaning, 'Wait until you depart before praising your host's entertainment,' (i.e. things may not end as pleasantly as they have begun).

41. stomachs appetites (i.e. for fresh food after a long sea-journey, and after their recent exhausting wandering on the island).

42. taste sample, try.

44–6. * mountaineers ... flesh Gonzalo describes goitre, a condition affecting people living in mountainous regions where there is a lack of iodine in the water, producing heavily-swollen flesh around the neck. (They looked like bulls which have a fold of loose skin hanging from their throats.)

46–7. * such ... breasts i.e. the Anthropophagi, mentioned in Mandeville's book of travels (written in the 14th century), and still half-believed in during Shakespeare's time.

48. * Each ... for one i.e. each traveller who insured himself before departure by *putting-out* (investing) money with an underwriter; on his return, and provided that he could prove that he had reached his destination, he could claim five times the sum invested from the underwriter (who kept what the traveller had 'put-out' or invested, if he did not return).

49. Good warrant of sure proof of.

49. stand to take your place at table (with perhaps a sense also of 'making a stand when', 'at bay': this point in the action is the point of no return for Alonso). Note the conclusive couplet-rhyming effect of '*feed ... last ... feel ... past*'.

51. * Brother ... Duke brother Sebastian, and you, my Lord Antonio, Duke of Milan.

52. do as we probably said as a courtesy (i.e. 'eat with me, the King') but possibly cautiously (i.e. to prove that they have not poisoned the food) if he suspects a plot against himself. (See note to Act II, Scene i, line 305.)

Stage Direction. **harpy** Ariel's appearance as one of the Furies of classical myth, divine messengers of vengeance, contrasts with his next appearance as presenter of the gracious Masque, In this scene and in the Masque spectacular devices are used.

Stage Direction. **claps his wings** perhaps to conceal the table for a moment to cover the disappearance of the food by a *quaint device* (ingenious mechanism). The banquet possibly disappears into the table by means of a false top.

53. three men of sin an unholy trinity, perhaps reminiscent of the three witches in *Macbeth*.

53–6. * whom ... up you whom Fate, which uses for its purposes this earth and all that it contains, has made the ocean, insatiable as it is, to spew you up (i.e. the sea accepts everything, but you turn its stomach).

56–8. * and on ... to live i.e. Destiny has marooned you on this desert island (the fate accorded to uncooperative sailors).

Such shapes, such gesture, and such sound,
    expressing,
Although they want the use of tongue, a kind
Of excellent dumb discourse.
Prospero [Aside]   Praise in departing.
Francisco
  They vanish'd strangely.
Sebastian   No matter, since   40
  They have left their viands behind; for we have
    stomachs.
Will't please you taste of what is here?
Alonso   Not I.
Gonzalo
  Faith, sir, you need not fear. When we were boys,
  Who would believe that there were mountaineers,
  Dewlapp'd like bulls, whose throats had hanging at
    'em   45
  Wallets of flesh? or that there were such men
  Whose heads stood in their breasts? which now we
    find
  Each putter-out of five for one will bring us
  Good warrant of.
Alonso   I will stand to, and feed,   50
  Although my last; no matter, since I feel
  The best is past. Brother, my lord the Duke,
  Stand to, and do as we.

  [Thunder and lightning. Enter ARIEL, like a harpy;
  claps his wings upon the table; and, with a quaint
        device, the banquet vanishes]

Ariel
  You are three men of sin, whom Destiny,
  That hath to instrument this lower world
  And what is in't, the never-surfeited sea   55
  Hath caus'd to belch up you; and on this island
  Where man doth not inhabit – you 'mongst men
  Being most unfit to live. I have made you mad;

58–60. * I have ... selves I have driven you out of your minds, and you are now behaving in the wild and reckless fashion (*suchlike valour*) of men who will stop at nothing, even at killing (*hang and drown*) themselves (*their ... selves*). (In *hang and drown* there is a reminder of the Boatswain, Act I, Scene i, perhaps.)

Stage Direction. *** draw ... swords** this action reminds us of Ferdinand's response to Prospero (Act I, Scene ii, lines 466–74), but the reasons for the actions are strongly contrasted.

61. ministers of Fate i.e. not mere 'ministers of the crown' performing the earthly commands of Alonso.

61–2. * elements ... temper'd i.e. Ariel and his colleagues are composed of the 'spiritual' elements of air and fire, the *means* by which the *material* of the swords (earth) were tempered (forged). Their swords can no more wound the winds or kill the waves than they can harm Ariel physically.

63–4. loud winds accusing voices of the winds (i.e they cannot be silenced by being wounded).

63–4. still-closing always closing up again (with perhaps the sense of closing-in for the kill as vengeful waters pouring scorn on the wild stabbing thrusts of their cornered prey).

65. dowle feather.

65. plume crest (i.e. part of his Harpy's helmet or head-dress).

66. like in the same way.

67. massy heavy. (Ariel 'freezes' them into immobility just as Prospero did Ferdinand.)

71. * sea ... requit it the sea has paid you back for the deed (when you exposed Prospero and Miranda to drowning).

74. Incens'd enraged.

74. all the creatures all created beings, all creation.

75. peace both 'inner peace of mind and spirit', and also the sense of physical peace (in that they are like kingdoms being invaded by avenging *powers*, as at the end of *Macbeth* when *the powers above Put on their instruments* in support of the soldiers waging their crusading war against Macbeth).

76. pronounce i.e. judgment. Ariel's speech is that of a law-court, in which the three guilty men are charged and sentenced.

77. Ling'ring perdition drawn-out sense of loss (of Ferdinand). (With perhaps the idea also that Alonso will be 'lost' and forgotten by the world in his long imprisonment, serving his life sentence.)

77–8. * worse ... at once worse than immediate execution.

78. step by step a reminder of Nemesis, the classical figure of vengeance sent by the gods to punish offenders, who hobbled slowly but inexorably after her victims.

78. attend wait upon you like attendants at court. (Ariel uses the word with fine irony: this is not the sort of 'attention' Alonso wants to have.)

79. your ways wherever you may go, till the end of your days. The image of wandering – like the Jew or like Cain with the mark of his brother's murder on his brow – repeats that of their *maze trod* through the labyrinthine paths of the island.

And even with such-like valour men hang and
drown
Their proper selves.

[ALONSO, SEBASTIAN etc., draw their swords]

                You fools! I and my fellows   60
Are ministers of Fate; the elements
Of whom your swords are temper'd may as well
Wound the loud winds, or with bemock'd-at stabs
Kill the still-closing waters, as diminish
One dowle that's in my plume; my fellow-ministers   65
Are like invulnerable. If you could hurt,
Your swords are now too massy for your strengths
And will not be uplifted. But remember –
For that's my business to you – that you three
From Milan did supplant good Prospero;   70
Expos'd unto the sea, which hath requit it,
Him, and his innocent child; for which foul deed
The pow'rs, delaying, not forgetting, have
Incens'd the seas and shores, yea, all the creatures,
Against your peace. Thee of thy son, Alonso,   75
They have bereft; and do pronounce by me
Ling'ring perdition, worse than any death
Can be at once, shall step by step attend
You and your ways; whose wraths to guard you
      from –

79–82. * **whose wraths ... ensuing** there is nothing to protect you from the wrath of the avenging powers, which would otherwise descend upon your heads here in this remote desert island, except the penance of a contrite heart, and an unblemished life in the future.

Stage Direction. **thunder** Ariel disappears as he came, to discordant and dramatic thunder. By contrast, the strange *shapes* remove the table to soft music (perhaps now felt to be mocking them as it accompanies the *shapes* who now use *mocks and mows*, grinning grimaces, in place of their previous *gentle actions of salutation*).

83. Bravely splendidly. (Perhaps Ariel is now *on the top* beside his master.)

84. * **a grace ... devouring** an absorbing grace, elegance.

85. bated left out.

86. hadst to say Prospero, the 'producer', has given Ariel a part to learn and to play.

87. observation strange unusual precision (rare exactness in following my instructions).

87. meaner lesser, lower.

88. * **several ... done** have played their particular parts.

88. high great.

89. knit up bound up. (Strongly ironical: *knit*, in Shakespeare, is commonly a binding in harmonious amity, and here Prospero's enemies allied against him, are only united in discordant madness, their *distractions*, and therefore made helpless.)

94–5. * Only the *three men of sin* have heard Ariel's words, and Gonzalo is horrified at his master's frenzied expression.

95. it is monstrous i.e. his sin (crime against Prospero) is horribly unnatural.

96–9. * **spoke ... sing ... pronounc'd ... bass** the imagery of these lines perhaps suggests the Service of Commination ('the denouncing of God's anger and judgements against sinners').

96–9. billows waves.

98–9. * **deep ... Prosper** a fine line and a half of expressive alliteration and assonance.

98–9. dreadful awe-inspiring.

98–9. pronounc'd compare line 76.

99. bass my trespass i.e. the thunder in uttering (*pronounced*) Prospero's name supplied the bass notes, or musical 'ground' to the whole harmony of natural sounds which are declaring Alonso's guilt (*trespass*).

100. Therefore for this reason (i.e. Alonso's crime).

101. * This suicidal line of Alonso's is almost identical with Prospero's in Act V, Scene i, line 56, but also in direct contrast to it: whereas Alonso is in despair and wishes to bury the past by dying, Prospero is burying the past with his magical equipment in the hope of a better future.

101. e'er plummet sounded than any ship's lead-line ever descended in sounding depths of water.

100–2. * **bedded ... sounded ... mudded** these three 'dead' (-ded) endings express a hopeless finality.

Which here, in this most desolate isle, else falls   80
Upon your heads – is nothing but heart's sorrow,
And a clear life ensuing.

[He vanishes in thunder; then, to soft music, enter
the SHAPES again, and dance, with mocks and mows,
and carrying out the table]

Prospero
Bravely the figure of this harpy hast thou
Perform'd, my Ariel; a grace it had, devouring.
Of my instruction hast thou nothing bated   85
In what thou hadst to say; so, with good life
And observation strange, my meaner ministers
Their several kinds have done. My high charms
        work,
And these mine enemies are all knit up
In their distractions. They now are in my pow'r;   90
And in these fits I leave them, while I visit
Young Ferdinand, whom they suppose is drown'd,
And his and mine lov'd darling.

[Exit above]

Gonzalo
I' th' name of something holy, sir, why stand you
In this strange stare?
Alonso
                    O, it is monstrous, monstrous!   95
Methought the billows spoke, and told me of it;
The winds did sing it to me; and the thunder,
That deep and dreadful organ-pipe, pronounc'd
The name of Prosper; it did bass my trespass.
Therefore my son i' th' ooze is bedded; and   100
I'll seek him deeper than e'er plummet sounded,
And with him there lie mudded.

[Exit]

103. * I'll fight ... o'er I'll fight their legions one after the other. (Compare Stephano's reaction in Act III, Scene ii, line 127.)

104. desperate frantic, reckless.

105. * Like ... after i.e. a poison with a delayed action (like a time-bomb) which did its work long after being given to a victim. (The poison simile is apt in that Italy was generally considered the place for sophisticated drugs and poisons at the time.)

106. bite the spirits prick their conscience. (This image is reversed in Act II, Scene ii, line 10, where Prospero's spirits *bite* Caliban.)

108. ecstasy madness, frenzy.

The tension of the play has been increasing as each of the three situations has brought its part of the plot to a climax. Now with the violent and stormy conclusion to the scene, and Alonso's headlong departure to seek Ferdinand *i' the ooze* reminding us of the tempest and the abandoning of the ship with which the play began, the calm harmonies of the Masque in Act IV come as a relief, a restoration of order which foreshadows the final reconciliation with which the play ends.

Sebastian   But one fiend at a time,
 I'll fight their legions o'er.
Antonio   I'll be thy second.

  [Exeunt SEBASTIAN and ANTONIO]

Gonzalo
 All three of them are desperate; their great guilt,
 Like poison given to work a great time after,   105
 Now gins to bite the spirits. I do beseech you,
 That are of suppler joints, follow them swiftly,
 And hinder them from what this ecstasy
 May now provoke them to.
Adrian   Follow, I pray you.

  [Exeunt]

ACT IV

Scene I

In Act IV Prospero begins to return to the foreground of the action: the royal group are safely *knit up in their distractions* and the comic trio are in the stagnant pool. He can afford time for an interlude during which he presents his Masque as a betrothal celebration for Ferdinand and Miranda and as a fine exhibition of his magical powers shortly before he relinquishes them. The short episode at the end of the Act, in which Caliban and his confederates are exposed, provides a relaxation from the serious level of action, a coming down to earth from the rarefied atmosphere of the Masque before rising again to the high poetry of the confrontation of Prospero and his enemies in Act V.

1. too austerely punished 'treated you too harshly' (in testing him).

3. third possibly a misprint in the Folio edition for 'thrid' (thread). Miranda being one of the essential strands in his beings. If it is *third*, then perhaps Milan and Prospero himself are the other two thirds.

5. tender offer.

5. vexations troubles, afflictions. (The word suggests turbulent agitation of minds and waters, as in Act I, Scene ii, line 229 *still-vex'd Bermoothes*, and of the mind as in Act IV, Scene i, line 158.)

7. strangely wonderfully well.

8. ratify confirm, bless (perhaps by placing Miranda's hand in Ferdinand's and holding both in his).

9. boast her off praise her highly.

11. halt come limping along (well behind her in the 'race' in which she will *outstrip*, or leave behind, anything which tries to keep up with her – in this case, praise).

12. Against an oracle against a declaration by an infallible source of truth to the contrary. (The most famous of oracles was the Delphic Oracle in Ancient Greece, to which people went to receive inspired utterance from the Pythia, a priestess of Apollo, god of wisdom.)

13–14. gift Ferdinand is given Miranda as a rich gift (i.e. a dowry in herself) by Prospero because he has deserved her: he has earned the right to possess her by worthily standing the test imposed on him.

15. * break ... knot go to bed with her, take away her virginity. (*Virgin-knot:* the girdle worn by maidens before marriage, in ancient times.) King James's view of the importance of chastity can be seen in a sentence from his *Basilikon Doron* (1599), a treatise on the arts of government: 'Be not ashamed then, to keepe cleane your body, which is the Temple of the holy Spirit.'

16. sanctimonious holy, sacred.

ACT FOUR

SCENE I. Before Prospero's cell.

[Enter PROSPERO, FERDINAND, and MIRANDA]

Prospero
  If I have too austerely punish'd you,
  Your compensation makes amends; for I
  Have given you here a third of mine own life,
  Or that for which I live; who once again
  I tender to thy hand. All thy vexations   5
  Were but my trials of thy love, and thou
  Hast strangely stood the test; here, afore heaven,
  I ratify this my rich gift. O Ferdinand!
  Do not smile at me that I boast her off,
  For thou shalt find she will outstrip all praise,   10
  And make it halt behind her.
Ferdinand
                              I do believe it
  Against an oracle.
Prospero
  Then, as my gift, and thine own acquisition
  Worthily purchas'd, take my daughter. But
  If thou dost break her virgin-knot before   15
  All sanctimonious ceremonies may

18–19. * **No sweet … grow** there are two interwoven ideas here: (a) the heavens (gods) will only bless the marriage and make it honourably fruitful if the proper ritual is observed, and (b) the heavens (skies) will only send fertilizing showers to produce a fruitful crop if the proper ritual is observed.

18–19. aspersion sprinkling (a) of dew, (b) in the Catholic ritual of the 'asperges', when the holy water is sprinkled.

19. contract betrothal.

19. barren hate referring (a) to the hateful barrenness of the soil, (b) hatred of each other for not being able to produce children.

20. Sour-eyed bitter looks of *disdain:* anger, scorn.

20–1. * **bestrew … weeds** referring both to the weeds which will spring up in place of a fruitful crop, and to the strewing of a marriage-bed with flowers (i.e. instead of a bridal bed being 'decked' with flowers to signify sweet fruitfulness it will be strewn with weeds, sour and unfruitful).

22–3. * **Therefore … light on you** Therefore be careful to restrain yourselves, if you hope to receive the blessing of the god of marriage.

22–3. Hymen Roman god of marriage, depicted bearing a torch.

24. fair issue fine children (i.e. not malformed like Caliban).

25. murkiest darkest, most ill-lit.

25. den hole, remote corner.

26. opportune convenient.

26. suggestion temptation.

27. * **Our … can** my evil spirit can offer. (A reference to the idea that each human soul had a good angel and a bad angel, the latter being its *worser genius*, fighting for possession of it.)

27–8. * **shall … lust** shall never reduce my honourable intentions to mere animal passion.

28–9. * **to take … celebration** so that the keen pleasure of my wedding-day is reduced.

30–1. * **When … below** when I shall imagine that the sun-god's chariot horses have gone lame, or that night has been chained in its dungeon below the world (i.e. Ferdinand in his eagerness for his nuptial night will think that the day is never going to end or the night to begin).

32. Sit, then i.e. like the royal couple they are, at a royal entertainment (e.g. a play or a masque in the Banqueting Hall of Whitehall).

32. talk with her presumably so that they are absorbed in each other while Prospero speaks to Ariel, (compare also Act III, Scene i, lines 57–9 when Miranda speaks of her father's *precept* not to speak too much to Ferdinand). They are silenced by Prospero at line 59 (see note).

33. What Come here!

35. meaner fellows lesser companions.

37. trick pageant-device (i.e. comparable with that of the banquet-scene).

37. rabble inferior spirits.

39. * **Incite … motion** make them get a move on.

41. vanity trifling exhibition (i.e. perhaps in comparison with the demonstration of power in raising the storm).

42. Presently? immediately?

43. twink twinkling of an eye.

With full and holy rite be minister'd,
No sweet aspersion shall the heavens let fall
To make this contract grow; but barren hate,
Sour-ey'd disdain, and discord, shall bestrew   20
The union of your bed with weeds so loathly
That you shall hate it both. Therefore take heed,
As Hymen's lamps shall light you.

Ferdinand   As I hope
For quiet days, fair issue, and long life,
With such love as 'tis now, the murkiest den,   25
The most opportune place, the strong'st suggestion
Our worser genius can, shall never melt
Mine honour into lust, to take away
The edge of that day's celebration,
When I shall think or Phoebus' steeds are founder'd   30
Or Night kept chain'd below.

Prospero   Fairly spoke.
Sit, then, and talk with her; she is thine own.
What, Ariel! my industrious servant, Ariel!

[Enter ARIEL]

Ariel
What would my potent master? Here I am

Prospero
Thou and thy meaner fellows your last service   35
Did worthily perform; and I must use you
In such another trick. Go bring the rabble,
O'er whom I give thee pow'r, here to this place.
Incite them to quick motion; for I must
Bestow upon the eyes of this young couple   40
Some vanity of mine art; it is my promise,
And they expect it from me.

Ariel   Presently?

Prospero
Ay, with a twink.

Ariel
              Before you can say 'come' and 'go,'
              And breathe twice, and cry 'so, so,'   45

46. tripping lightly dancing.

47. mop and mow presumably these grimaces would be in contrast to the sneering ones of Act III, Scene iii, line 83 (stage direction).

50. I conceive I understand, 'I get you'.

51. true i.e. to your promise (to be restrained).

51. dalliance love-making.

52. Too much the rein too much freedom, too little restraint.

52–3. * oaths ... blood the most solemn vows are as inflammable as straw when burning passion rages between two people.

55–6. * The white ... liver either (a) Miranda's chaste maidenly white breast leaning upon my chest calms my passions, or (b) the pure image of the virginal Miranda in my heart cools my heated passion. (Both images are simultaneously possible.)

57. corollary extra spirits (i.e. too many rather than too few).

58. pertly briskly, promptly.

59. * No ... silent i.e. so that the spell of the magical Masque will not be broken.

Stage Direction. **Enter Iris** Iris was the classical literature goddess of the rainbow and messenger of the gods and symbolized peace. As the rainbow she links Juno (Queen of Heaven) with Ceres (Queen of Earth).

60. bounteous generous, liberal.

60. leas meadows.

61. vetches small cattle-fodder vegetable.

61. pease peas.

63. meads meadows.

63. stover winter cattle-fodder.

64. pioned and twilled probably a description of banks dug by pioneers (i.e. diggers, trenchers) who then 'twill' the 'brims', i.e. strengthen the top edges by revetting or lining them with criss-crossed branches.

65. hest command.

66. * cold ... crowns the fresh-water spirits (of the full streams of springtime) have maidens' coronets made of *pioned and twill'd brims*.

66. broom groves some editors read 'brown groves' (i.e. shady), though a sulking lover could possibly hide among broom (gorse) bushes growing in *groves*.

68. lass-lorn rejected by his sweetheart.

68. pole-clipt probably 'poll-clipt', i.e. pollarded or pruned grape-vines in the spring.

69. sea-marge coastline, at the margin or edge of the sea.

69. sterile i.e. in contrast to the images of potential fertility in the previous lines.

Each one, tripping on his toe,
Will be here with mop and mow.
Do you love me, master? No?

Prospero
Dearly, my delicate Ariel. Do not approach
Till thou dost hear me call.

Ariel   Well! I conceive.   50

[Exit]

Prospero
Look thou be true; do not give dalliance
Too much the rein; the strongest oaths are straw
To th' fire i' th' blood. Be more abstemious,
Or else good night your vow!

Ferdinand   I warrant you, sir,
The white cold virgin snow upon my heart   55
Abates the ardour of my liver.

Prospero   Well!
Now come, my Ariel, bring a corollary,
Rather than want a spirit; appear, and pertly.
No tongue! All eyes! Be silent.

[Soft music.
Enter IRIS]

Iris
Ceres, most bounteous lady, thy rich leas   60
Of wheat, rye, barley, vetches, oats, and pease;
Thy turfy mountains, where live nibbling sheep,
And flat meads thatch'd with stover, them to keep;
Thy banks with pioned and twilled brims,
Which spongy April at thy hest betrims,   65
To make cold nymphs chaste crowns; and thy
          broom groves,
Whose shadow the dismissed bachelor loves,
Being lass-lorn; thy pole-clipt vineyard;
And thy sea-marge, sterile and rocky-hard,

70. air Ceres 'take the air' at the edge of the land, refreshes herself at the seaside.

70. * Queen ... sky Juno.

71. wat'ry arch rainbow.

72. these i.e. your domain (described in Iris's speech).

74. peacocks peacocks were sacred to Juno (as doves were to Venus, see line 94), and drew her chariot.

74. amain swiftly.

Stage Direction. **Juno descends** either from the Heavens, the projecting roof over the apron stage of the public playhouse, in which case she would be lowered by machinery, or from the raised level of the rear stage if at an indoor performance. In either case the movement is slow since she does not reach the main stage until line 101.

75. * Approach ... entertain Iris, like a royal harbinger, precedes her sovereign lady, Juno, and summons the lesser deity, Ceres, to await her monarch's arrival (as an Elizabethan noble might wait on his land to greet and entertain his Queen during one of her 'progresses').

78. saffron orange-red.

79. Diffusest honey drops spreads sweet rain-drops.

80–1. * And with ... scarf i.e. one end of the rainbow rests upon Ceres's shrubbed or wooded (*bosky*) land, and the other upon her bare uplands, like a richly-coloured scarf.

83. short-grassed green perhaps not simply suggesting a lawn, but also a reference to the green-baize covering of the floor of the inner stage at Whitehall.

85. estate bestow.

86. heavenly bow rainbow.

88–91. * Since ... forsworn since they (Venus, goddess of sexual love, and her blind son, Cupid) devised the plan by which dark Dis (Pluto, King of the Underworld, or Hades) seized my daughter Persephone (Proserpine) to be his bride, I have given up having anything to do with such a notorious pair (i.e. as Venus and Cupid).

91. Of her society of her company, (i.e. of meeting her).

93. Paphos chief shrine to Venus (a town in Cyprus).

94. * Compare line 74, and note.

94–7. * Here ... lighted i.e. Venus and Cupid have withdrawn, defeated, having thought to lure Ferdinand and Miranda (by means of a *wanton charm* = lascivious spell) to break the vow they took to remain chaste, and not sleep together before their wedding-night.

98. Mars's hot minion i.e. Venus, the lustful mistress of Mars, the god of war.

98. is return'd again has gone back to Paphos.

Where thou thyself dost air – the Queen o' th' sky,   70
Whose wat'ry arch and messenger am I,
Bids thee leave these; and with her sovereign grace,
Here on this grass-plot, in this very place,
To come and sport. Her peacocks fly amain.

[JUNO descends in her car. Approach, rich Ceres, her
        to entertain. Enter CERES]

Ceres
Hail, many-coloured messenger, that ne'er   75
Dost disobey the wife of Jupiter;
Who, with thy saffron wings, upon my flow'rs
Diffusest honey drops, refreshing show'rs;
And with each end of thy blue bow dost crown
My bosky acres and my unshrubb'd down,   80
Rich scarf to my proud earth – why hath thy Queen
Summon'd me hither to this short-grass'd green?
Iris
A contract of true love to celebrate,
And some donation freely to estate   85
On the blest lovers.
Ceres   Tell me, heavenly bow,
If Venus or her son, as thou dost know,
Do now attend the Queen? Since they did plot
The means that dusky Dis my daughter got,
Her and her blind boy's scandal'd company   90
I have forsworn.
Iris   Of her society
Be not afraid. I met her Deity
Cutting the clouds towards Paphos, and her son
Dove-drawn with her. Here thought they to have done
Some wanton charm upon this man and maid,   95
Whose vows are that no bed-rite shall be paid
Till Hymen's torch be lighted; but in vain.
Mars's hot minion is return'd again;

99. waspish-headed son i.e. Cupid, whose arrows sting waspishly, peevishly.

99. broke his arrows i.e. in a fit of temper because chastity has triumphed.

100. sparrows sacred to Venus; and like her doves, symbolizing amorousness and lechery.

101. a boy right out simply a boy.

101. of State stately.

102. gait the way she walks (i.e. in a stately manner).

103. Go with me Juno, protector of married couples, goes to bless the engaged couple with spiritual gifts, and Ceres to bless them with material ones.

105. issue children.

108. still ever, always.

110. foison abundance.

110. increase produce, crops.

111. garners granaries, barns for grain.

106–13. * Juno's words are largely abstract (e.g. *honour, riches, marriage-blessing, continuance, joys, blessings*) as suits her spiritual role; Ceres' are concrete (e.g. *earth, foison, barns, garners, vines, bunches, plants*) to suit her material role.

114–15. * **Spring ... harvest** Ceres has given a vision of Golden Age abundance, and now imagines Spring immediately following the late-summer harvest so that the lovers will experience no winter in their paradisal happiness. (This would always happen if Dis had not carried off Persephone and so brought winter into the world. See line 89.)

117. so to this end.

119. Harmonious charmingly music has cast its spell (*charmingly:* i.e. as a charm) upon the ear just as the spectacular *vision* has upon the eye.

123. a wonder'd father (a) an amazing father (i.e. to be wondered at), (b) a father capable of working wonders.

123. and a wise *wise* provides a rhyme for *Paradise*, but may be a misprint for 'wife', in which case Miranda (*O you wonder*, Act I, Scene ii, line 427) completes the picture of an Eden-island, with God-the-Father-Prospero, Adam-Ferdinand, and Eve-Miranda.

Her waspish-headed son has broke his arrows,
Swears he will shoot no more, but play with   100
    sparrows,
And be a boy right out.

            [JUNO alights]

Ceres   Highest Queen of State,
Great Juno, comes; I know her by her gait.
Juno
How does my bounteous sister? Go with me
To bless this twain, that they may prosperous be,
And honour'd in their issue.   105

          [They sing]

Juno   Honour, riches, marriage-blessing,
         Long continuance, and increasing,
         Hourly joys be still upon you!
         Juno sings her blessings on you.
Ceres   Earth's increase, foison plenty,   110
         Barns and garners never empty;
         Vines with clust'ring bunches growing,
         Plants with goodly burden bowing;
         Spring come to you at the farthest,
         In the very end of harvest!   115
         Scarcity and want shall shun you,
         Ceres' blessing so is on you.
Ferdinand
This is a most majestic vision, and
Harmonious charmingly. May I be bold
To think these spirits?
Prospero   Spirits, which by mine art   120
I have from their confines call'd to enact
My present fancies.
Ferdinand
           Let me live here ever;
So rare a wonder'd father and a wise
Makes this place Paradise.

126. * **There's … to do** there's more about to happen.
127. **marr'd** spoilt (compare line 59).
128. **Naiads** water-nymphs.
128. **windring** a combination of 'winding' and 'wandering'.
129. **sedg'd** reedy, with rushes growing.
130. **crisp** rippled.
130. **this green land** see note to line 83.
132. **temperate** chaste, cool.

134–8. sun-burnt sicklemen etc. the hot and earthy male reapers meet (*encounter* often has sexual connotations in Shakespeare) the chaste nymphs in a rustic dance (*country footing*), a fertility ritual. In the meeting of April nymphs (see line 65) and August harvesters, water and earth, and Spring and late-Summer harvest, are united.

   Stage Direction. **starts** seems startled, alarmed.
   Stage Direction. **hollow** reverberating.
   Stage Direction. **heavily** sadly, mournfully.

142. **avoid** 'away with you!' (spoken to Juno, Iris, Ceres).
143. **passion** powerful emotion, anger.

144. **works** moves, disturbs, (he is 'getting worked up').
145. **distemper'd** vexed, upset (out of an even temper).

[JUNO and CERES whisper and send IRIS on
employment]

Prospero   Sweet now, silence;
  Juno and Ceres whisper seriously.   125
  There's something else to do; hush, and be mute,
  Or else our spell is marr'd.
Iris
  You nymphs, call'd Naiads, of the wind'ring brooks,
  With your sedg'd crowns and ever harmless looks,
  Leave your crisp channels, and on this green land   130
  Answer your summons; Juno does command.
  Come, temperate nymphs, and help to celebrate
  A contract of true love; be not too late.

[Enter certain NYMPHS]

  You sun-burnt sicklemen, of August weary,
  Come hither from the furrow, and be merry;   135
  Make holiday; your rye-straw hats put on,
  And these fresh nymphs encounter every one
  In country footing.

    [Enter certain REAPERS, properly habited; they
    join with the NYMPHS in a graceful dance;
    towards the end whereof PROSPERO starts
    suddenly, and speaks; after which, to a strange,
    hollow, and confused noise, they heavily vanish]

Prospero [Aside]
  I had forgot that foul conspiracy
  Of the beast Caliban and his confederates   140
  Against my life; the minute of their plot
  Is almost come. [To the SPIRITS] Well done; avoid;
  no more!
Ferdinand
  This is strange; your father's in some passion
  That works him strongly.
Miranda   Never till this day
  Saw I him touch'd with anger so distemper'd.   145

146. in a mov'd sort troubled, diconcerted.

148. revels entertainment.

149. As I foretold you presumably Prospero both promised (see line 41) and *foretold* between the end of Act III, Scene i, and the beginning of Act IV.

151. baseless fabric cloth which has no 'base' or 'ground' and therefore no substantiality.

151–6. this vision Prospero describes the transcience of human beings, their most splendid and apparently permanent achievements, and the world itself, in terms of actors, masque scenery, and pageant equipment which is dismantled and disappears after the performance.

154. all which it inherit everything which this vision possesses.

155. * this ... pageant this masque, which is pure illusion.

156. not a rack no trace (literally, not a cloud). There is a suggestion of 'stage-clouds' (i.e. scenery).

156. stuff material (perhaps connecting with *fabric* in line 151).

157. on of.

158. rounded rounded off, completed (perhaps 'brought full circle'), crowned.

158. vex'd agitated.

159. weakness i.e. that I should be so upset, not better able to control my feelings (of anger at the *foul conspiracy*).

163. beating i.e. agitated, restless (like the sea beating on the shore), pulsating. (Compare Act I, Scene ii, line 176.)

165. I cleave to I cling to, am inseparably part of.

166. meet with (a) confront, (b) settle our account with, (c) deal with.

167. * When ... Ceres either (a) when I represented (i.e. acted the part of) Ceres, or (b) when I introduced Ceres in the masque (perhaps himself playing Iris).

170. varlets rascals, knaves.

Prospero
    You do look, my son, in a mov'd sort,
    As if you were dismay'd; be cheerful, sir.
    Our revels now are ended. These our actors,
    As I foretold you, were all spirits, and
    Are melted into air, into thin air;   150
    And, like the baseless fabric of this vision,
    The cloud-capp'd towers, the gorgeous palaces,
    The solemn temples, the great globe itself,
    Yea, all which it inherit, shall dissolve,
    And, like this insubstantial pageant faded,   155
    Leave not a rack behind. We are such stuff
    As dreams are made on; and our little life
    Is rounded with a sleep. Sir, I am vex'd;
    Bear with my weakness; my old brain is troubled;
    Be not disturb'd with my infirmity.   160
    If you be pleas'd, retire into my cell
    And there repose; a turn or two I'll walk
    To still my beating mind.
Ferdinand and Miranda   We wish your peace.

[Exeunt]

Prospero
    Come, with a thought. I thank thee, Ariel; come.

[Enter ARIEL]

Ariel
    Thy thoughts I cleave to. What's thy pleasure?
Prospero   Spirit,   165
    We must prepare to meet with Caliban.
Ariel
    Ay, my commander. When I presented Ceres,
    I thought to have told thee of it; but I fear'd
    Lest I might anger thee.
Prospero
    Say again, where didst thou leave these varlets?   170

172. valour 'Dutch courage' (i.e. given them by the wine).

174. * kissing ... feet a reminder of Caliban prostrating himself before Stephano in Act II, Scene ii, line 145, *I'll kiss thy foot*. (In smiting the air and beating the ground, they are behaving like irrational tyrants cruelly maltreating their subjects, some for simply daring to breathe in their presence and others for humbly seeking their favour in submissively kissing their feet.)

174. bending directing their course, heading for.

175. project purpose, objective (compare Act V, Scene i, line 1).

175. unback'd unbroken, never ridden.

176–7. * prick'd ... Advanc'd ... lifted up all three words mean much the same thing and exactly describe the action: first, the three 'animals' hear the drum, cocking their ears; then they look up to see where the sound is coming from; then they raise their muzzles as if to scent it. (Ariel probably imitates their actions throughout this graphic speech, as he does in true Messenger (or commentator) fashion in his other descriptions.)

179. calf-like perhaps a reminder of the *mooncalf*.

179. lowing Ariel's music was to them in their animal state like the mooing of the mother cow calling to them to follow her.

180. goss gorse.

182. filthy mantled covered with scum (filth).

183–4. * that ... feet so that (by disturbing the foul water) the pond smelt even worse than their feet did. (Rotting leaves at the bottom of a neglected pond create an unpleasant gas.)

**171–84. * The physical brutishness of the trio is vigorously conveyed by enumerating parts of the body (*faces, feet, unback'd, ears, eyelids, noses, ears, tooth'd, shins, chins, feet*) and by stressing movement (*drinking, smote, breathing, beat, kissing, bending* etc.).

184. bird suggesting Ariel's swiftness and free flight.

185. * A reminder to the audience that Ariel is only visible to Prospero.

186. trumpery showy materials.

187. stale (a) bait (literally, a decoy bird) but also perhaps (b) a whore (to lure them in her gaudy gear).

188–90. devil, devil, all, all lost, the repetitions convey the mixture of anger and regret Prospero feels at having failed (magician as he is, he can only control the physical world) and stress his failure.

189. nurture education, training, upbringing. (Without the externally imposed discipline of *nurture*, man is no more than a beast and lacking in dignity and self-control.)

189–90. * my pains ... taken all my efforts made out of kindness.

191. age with each passing year.

192. cankers grows more malignant, corrupted, infected with evil.

191–2. * body ... mind the Platonic idea that the body and the mind resemble each other is also expressed in Miranda's description of Ferdinand (Act I, Scene ii, line 458).

Ariel

    I told you, sir, they were red-hot with drinking;
    So full of valour that they smote the air
    For breathing in their faces; beat the ground
    For kissing of their feet; yet always bending
    Towards their project. Then I beat my tabor,   175
    At which like unback'd colts they prick'd their ears,
    Advanc'd their eyelids, lifted up their noses
    As they smelt music; so I charm'd their ears,
    That calf-like they my lowing follow'd through
    Tooth'd briers, sharp furzes, pricking goss, and
        thorns,   180
    Which enter'd their frail shins. At last I left them
    I' th' filthy mantled pool beyond your cell,
    There dancing up to th' chins, that the foul lake
    O'erstunk their feet.

Prospero   This was well done, my bird.
    Thy shape invisible retain thou still.   185
    The trumpery in my house, go bring it hither
    For stale to catch these thieves.

Ariel   I go, I go.

              [Exit]

Prospero

    A devil, a born devil, on whose nature
    Nurture can never stick; on whom my pains,
    Humanely taken, all, all lost, quite lost;   190
    And as with age his body uglier grows,
    So his mind cankers. I will plague them all,
    Even to roaring.

Stage Direction. **glistening apparel** i.e. the *trumpery* (line 186). Like children, they are attracted by bright, shining objects, and forget that 'All that glisters is not gold' (*Merchant of Venice*, Act II, Scene vii, line 65). However, since the *stuffs* came from Prospero's wardrobe, they might have been worn by him, or made up into dresses for Miranda; robes are only 'real gold' when worn by their rightful owners, otherwise they are mere show.

193. line either (a) clothes-line, or (b) lime-tree (see Act V, Scene i, line 10).

194. blind mole i.e. a creature with the most acute hearing listening just below them ('so softly that even...').

197. play'd the Jack (a) behaved like a knave, (b) been a misleading Jack o' Lantern, will o' th' wisp. (The will o' th' wisp, a light probably produced by marsh-gas, which led travellers astray by night and into boggy land, combines with the idea of a deceitful knave tricking them.)

199. horse-piss horse-urine (perhaps suggested by *stale* in line 187, which can mean urine).

202. displeasure i.e. 'King' Stephano will show his royal displeasure. Compare the phrase 'at the king's pleasure'. (The word may have some subconscious link for Shakespeare with evil-smelling ponds. In *All's Well* we find: *I am now, sir, muddied in fortune's mood, and smell somewhat strong of her displeasure*, and *the unclean fishpond of her displeasure*.)

204–5. * These words by Caliban could in another context be just those of a cringing courtier seeking a favour of his king.

206. hoodwink this mischance cover up this unfortunate episode (in the pool). (Hawks were 'hoodwinked', i.e. covered with a hood, making them harmless. Caliban wants his mistake made in calling Ariel a *harmless fairy* to be forgotten.)

209. disgrace and dishonour both words are suitable to nobles who have suffered a defeat.

211. That's more perhaps this is deliberately ambiguous, i.e. Trinculo is probably referring to the loss of the bottle, but would like to be thought to refer to the loss of his honour.

213. fetch off rescue, get back.

213. o'er ears totally immersed. (Perhaps Stephano starts to leave and is stopped by Caliban, who keeps him to his purpose by pointing out that they are at the entrance to the cell.) There may be a parallel between 'King' Stephano and King Alonso here: the former going to plunge into the pond for his lost bottle, the latter into the sea for his lost son.

[Re-enter ARIEL, loaden with glistering apparel]

Come, hang them on this line.

[PROSPERO and ARIEL remain, invisible]

[Enter CALIBAN, STEPHANO, and TRINCULO, all wet]

Caliban
Pray you, tread softly, that the blind mole may not
Hear a foot fall; we now are near his cell.   195
Stephano
Monster, your fairy, which you say is a harmless
fairy, has done little better than play'd the Jack with
us.
Trinculo
Monster, I do smell all horse-piss at which my nose
is in great indignation.   200
Stephano
So is mine. Do you hear, monster?
If I should take a displeasure against you, look you –
Trinculo
Thou wert but a lost monster.
Caliban
Good my lord, give me thy favour still.
Be patient, for the prize I'll bring thee to   205
Shall hoodwink this mischance; therefore speak softly.
All's hush'd as midnight yet.
Trinculo
Ay, but to lose our bottles in the pool!
Stephano
There is not only disgrace and dishonour in that,
monster, but an infinite loss.   210
Trinculo
That's more to me than my wetting; yet this is your
harmless fairy, monster.
Stephano
I will fetch off my bottle, though I be o'er ears for
my labour.

217. good mischief excellent crime. (An example of an oxymoron or para-doxical phrase.)

219. foot-licker Caliban is the very picture of obsequiousness. (Compare Act III, Scene ii, line 22, *lick thy foot,* and references to kissing feet. Licking is equivalent to 'sucking up' as is seen in *Hamlet,* Act III, Scene ii, line 65, *Let the candied tongue lick absurd pomp.*)

220. * Stephano's pompously theatrical words show him to be no man for deeds.

222. O King Stephano Trinculo is not, presumably, deliberately 'taking the mickey' out of Stephano, but the allusion to the Ballad of King Stephen would underline to the audience Stephano's poor claims to kingship: *King Stephen was a worthy peer, His breeches cost him but a crown,*

225. frippery old clothes shop.

225. * **O ... Stephano** Trinculo is no doubt parading in one of the flashier robes or pieces of material as he says this.

227. by this hand Stephano makes a threatening gesture (like the bully he is).

230. dropsy drown may this fool be drowned by the watery fluid in his own body. *dropsy* is a condition in which there is too much body fluid in a person, causing him to swell. (In *drown* there is another echo of death by water.)

231. luggage encumbering rubbish.

233. crown crown of the head (with an allusion to Stephano's royal crown, which he will usurp from Prospero).

234. Make us strange stuff i.e. we will be transformed by his tortures (*pinching*) into strange material (*stuff*) if we are diverted from our purpose by this *stuff.*

235–40. * Stephano and Trinculo are almost certainly exchanging obscene puns, accompanied perhaps by appropriate actions.

235. Mistress line spoken to the lime-tree or clothes-line as he takes the jerkin. (Could he be *singing* the words, *Mistress line, is not this my jerkin?* to the tune, *O Mistress mine where are you roaming?* from *Twelfth Night?*)

235. jerkin short jacket.

236. under the line (a) under the lime-tree, or (b) the clothes-line, or (c) the loin ('-oin' was pronounced '-ine' at the time), or (d) below the Equator (still referred to as 'line' in the phrase 'crossing the line').

237. lose your hair either (a) through fever (e.g. scurvy) contracted at the Equator, or (b) venereal disease.

238. Do, do 'Go on, go on!' (Either referring to Stephano's stealing, or to his succession of puns, or both.)

238. steal if steal is pronounced 'stale' (the '-ea' as in 'break') then Pros-pero's words in line 187 are recalled, and the loin-hair pun continued.

238. by line and level systematically. (The reference is to building, using a plumb-line for vertical and a level for horizontal accuracy, i.e. we steal according to rule'.)

238. an't like if it please.

Caliban

    Prithee, my king, be quiet. Seest thou here,   215
    This is the mouth o' th' cell; no noise, and enter.
    Do that good mischief which may make this island
    Thine own for ever, and I, thy Caliban,
    For aye thy foot-licker.

Stephano

    Give me thy hand. I do begin to have bloody   220
    thoughts.

Trinculo

    O King Stephano! O peer! O worthy Stephano!
    Look what a wardrobe here is for thee!

Caliban

    Let it alone, thou fool; it is but trash.

Trinculo

    O, ho, monster; we know what belongs to a   225
    frippery. O King Stephano!

Stephano

    Put off that gown, Trinculo; by this hand, I'll have
    that gown.

Trinculo

    Thy Grace shall have it.

Caliban

    The dropsy drown this fool! What do you mean   230
    To dote thus on such luggage? Let't alone,
    And do the murder first. If he awake,
    From toe to crown he'll fill our skins with pinches;
    Make us strange stuff.

Stephano

    Be you quiet, monster. Mistress line, is not this my   235
    jerkin? Now is the jerkin under the line; now, jerkin,
    you are like to lose your hair, and prove a bald jerkin.

Trinculo

    Do, do. We steal by line and level, an't like your
    Grace.

Stephano

    I thank thee for that jest; here's a garment for't. Wit   240

242–3. pass of pate 'crack', witty remark (lit. a thrust of wit).

244. lime bird-lime (used by thieves who coated branches with this sticky substance in order to catch birds).

246. none on't none of it, nothing to do with it.
246. time opportunity.
247. barnacles barnacle-geese. (Popular folklore said that ship's barnacles were metamorphosed into geese. Taken with *apes* this could be another example of the general theme of transformation, in this case into something lower in the order of natural beings.)
248. * foreheads ... low i.e. ugly, serflike lowbrows.
  Stage Direction. * This episode may correspond to an Anti-masque, a spectacular yet comic, earthy contrast to the dignified and supernatural Masque.

254–6. * Mountain ... Silver ... Fury ... Tyrant the names of the hounds in Prospero's spirit-pack.

257. charge command.
258. dry convulsions cramps, spasms (thought in Shakespeare's time to be caused by a deficiency in bodily fluids needed to lubricate the joints).
259. aged cramps old people's cramps.
259. pinch-spotted bruised (black and blue) with pinching.
260. pard panther.
260. cat o' mountain leopard.

shall not go unrewarded while I am king of this
country. 'Steal by line and level' is an excellent pass
of pate; there's another garment for't.

Trinculo

Monster, come, put some lime upon your fingers,
and away with the rest.   245

Caliban

I will have none on't. We shall lose our time,
And all be turn'd to barnacles, or to apes
With foreheads villainous low.

Stephano

Monster, lay-to your fingers; help to bear this away
where my hogshead of wine is, or I'll turn you out   250
of my kingdom. Go to, carry this.

Trinculo

And this.

Stephano

Ay, and this.

[A noise of hunters heard. Enter divers SPIRITS, in
shape of dogs and hounds, hunting them about;
PROSPERO and ARIEL setting them on]

Prospero

Hey, Mountain, hey!

Ariel

Silver! there it goes, Silver!   255

Prospero

Fury, Fury! There, Tyrant, there! Hark, hark!

[CALIBAN, STEPHANO, and TRINCULO are driven out]

Go charge my goblins that they grind their joints
With dry convulsions, shorten up their sinews
With aged cramps, and more pinch-spotted make
them
Than pard or cat o' mountain.

Ariel

                              Hark, they roar.   260

Since Act V will be largely occupied with Prospero's reconciliation with his enemies and the resignation of his Art, Shakespeare, using the device of a play within a play, gives most of Act IV to the marriage theme; for it is the lovers who are the future, and it is on them that a better life depends. The Masque, with its themes of self-control and fruitfulness, points the way to a better life.

Prospero
Let them be hunted soundly. At this hour
Lies at my mercy all mine enemies.
Shortly shall all my labours end, and thou
Shalt have the air at freedom; for a little
Follow, and do me service.   265

[Exeunt]

ACT V

SCENE I

The three strands of the plot are now gathered together; the paths trodden by the three groups meet at Prospero's cell. As *The Tempest* is not a tragedy of revenge but a romance comedy of reconciliation, Prospero performs the *rarer action* of pardoning his enemies: it is always easier to be vindictive than to forgive. In setting them free by forgiveness and releasing Ariel, he frees himself and his Art is no longer needed.

Stage Direction. **in his magic robes** the break between Acts IV and V is perhaps no longer than to allow Prospero to withdraw into his cell and reappear in his magic robes, which he has to put on in order formally to divest himself of them in the transformation during Ariel's song (lines 88–94).

1. project (a) undertaking, purpose, (b) 'projection', the experiment by which alchemists hoped to change base metal into gold by means of the 'philosopher's stone'. (Prospero's purpose in the play is to transform the characters and the situation with which it starts, to change them from base metal into gold.)

1. gather to a head (a) approach the crisis (of the experiment), (b) come to bursting-point (of a boil), when the corruption of the past will come into the open and be cleared.

2. charms crack not (a) spells remain unbroken, (b) the chemical retort has not exploded, ruining the experiment.

2–3. * time ... carriage there is little left to do. (Time is personified as someone now able to walk erect after shedding most of his burden, i.e. having discharged his duty, as Prospero has almost done.)

8. gave in charge instructed me.

10. line-grove lime-tree grove.

10. weather-fends shields from rough weather, storms.

11. budge till ... release move until you release them (i.e. give the order, like a magistrate, for their release).

16–17. * like ... reeds like winter rain dripping rapidly and steadily from the overhanging thatch of a cottage roof (i.e. jutting out like a beard). Compare note to Act I, Scene ii, line 213.

17. works 'em moves them (with remorse).

18. affections emotions, feelings.

8–19. * Ariel's descriptive speech, broken into slow, short phrases and sentences, not only persuades Prospero of his enemies' change of heart but prepares the audience to accept the transformation. Ariel's dramatic role is largely to prepare us for the next step in the action by telling Prospero of what has just happened.

ACT FIVE

SCENE I. Before Prospero's cell.

[Enter PROSPERO in his magic robes, and ARIEL]

Prospero
Now does my project gather to a head;
My charms crack not, my spirits obey; and time
Goes upright with his carriage. How's the day?
Ariel
On the sixth hour; at which time, my lord,
You said our work should cease.
Prospero
                  I did say so,   5
When first I rais'd the tempest. Say, my spirit,
How fares the King and 's followers?
Ariel   Confin'd together
In the same fashion as you gave in charge;
Just as you left them; all prisoners, sir,
In the line-grove which weather-fends your cell;   10
They cannot budge till your release. The King,
His brother, and yours, abide all three distracted,
And the remainder mourning over them,
Brim full of sorrow and dismay; but chiefly
Him you term'd, sir, 'the good old lord, Gonzalo';   15
His tears run down his beard, like winter's drops
From eaves of reeds. Your charm so strongly works
    'em
That if you now beheld them your affections
Would become tender.
Prospero   Dost thou think so, spirit?

20. And mine shall the three simple words are highly expressive of a firm decision.

21. a touch a sensitive awareness, delicate sympathy.

22–4. * shall not … thou art? shall I, a human being like them, experiencing everything as acutely as they do, and feeling it as sensitively, not be moved with more human sympathy towards them than you are?

25. high wrongs great injuries done to me.

25. * struck … quick the sharp sound of the words suggests the action of touching a nerve.

25. quick the sensitive flesh below the skin (and, taken with *struck*, also suggesting a sudden pain). There might also be a sense in which Prospero has been repeatedly lashed by their *high wrongs* so that the skin has been stripped and the tender flesh below exposed.

26–30. * Prospero chooses the way of forgiveness, nobler behaviour then that of (even righteous) anger; it is a finer course of action to do positive good than to take an easier, more 'natural' revenge. His whole aim has been, he says, to 'make it up' once he was sure that they were penitent, and once he has achieved this end there will be no more need for him to show any displeasure.

33–50. * Prospero's lines probably derive from Medea's incantation in Ovid's *Metamorphoses* (Book VII). Shakespeare may have worked both from the original Latin and from Golding's version, an English translation (1567). Comparison with the original shows how English Shakespeare made many of the details, from *demi-puppets* to *curfew*.

36. demi-puppets little elves.

37. green sour ringlets the 'fairy-rings' of darker grass in which toadstools grow, made by dancing fairies (according to folklore).

39–40. * midnight … curfew mushrooms appear only by night and are thus like spirits at liberty to appear on earth only between curfew and cock-crow, i.e. during the hours when man is indoors.

39–40. curfew the moment when household fires had to be damped down to reduce the risk of a conflagration. Cottagers would then go to bed, and the mushrooms could prepare to come out.

41. masters spirits.

41. be-dimm'd eclipsed.

42. * call'd … winds released the rebellious winds from their caves (their homes, according to classical myth, and in this context confinement from which they are set free; perhaps like mutineers). This is yet another image of release.

43. azur'd vault blue (over-arching) sky.

45. fire lightning. Possibly suggesting in *given fire*, the the *roaring war* image, the touching-off of cannon by a linstock.

45–6. * Jove's … bolt Jupiter's own thunderbolt is being used against him to split his own tree, the royal oak.

47. spurs roots. Perhaps continuing the battle image, with horsed knights up-ended by cannon-balls and explosions.

48. pine and cedar i.e. both tall trees, and perhaps also chosen for the alliterative 'p' and 's' sounds, following *strong … promontory … spurs pluck'd.*

Ariel
  Mine would, sir, were I human.
Prospero   And mine shall.   20
  Hast thou, which art but air, a touch, a feeling
  Of their afflictions, and shall not myself,
  One of their kind, that relish all as sharply,
  Passion as they, be kindlier mov'd than thou art?
  Though with their high wrongs I am struck to th'
          quick,   25
  Yet with my nobler reason 'gainst my fury
  Do I take part; the rarer action is
  In virtue than in vengeance; they being penitent,
  The sole drift of my purpose doth extend
  Not a frown further. Go release them, Ariel;   30
  My charms I'll break, their senses I'll restore,
  And they shall be themselves.
Ariel   I'll fetch them, sir.

                        [Exit]

Prospero
  Ye elves of hills, brooks, standing lakes, and groves;
  And ye that on the sands with printless foot
  Do chase the ebbing Neptune, and do fly him   35
  When he comes back; you demi puppets that
  By moonshine do the green sour ringlets make,
  Whereof the ewe not bites; and you whose pastime
  Is to make midnight mushrooms, that rejoice
  To hear the solemn curfew; by whose aid –   40
  Weak masters though ye be – I have be-dimm'd
  The noontide sun, call'd forth the mutinous winds,
  And 'twixt the green sea and the azur'd vault
  Set roaring war. To the dread rattling thunder
  Have I given fire, and rifted Jove's stout oak   45
  With his own bolt; the strong-bas'd promontory
  Have I made shake, and by the spurs pluck'd up
  The pine and cedar. Graves at my command
  Have wak'd their sleepers, op'd, and let 'em forth,

50. rough magic crudely material (physical) kind of magic (in contrast to the more difficult and subtle power of transforming men's minds), using the elements of fire, air, water, earth. (See note to Act I, Scene ii, lines 1–13.)

51. abjure remounce.

51. requir'd requested.

53. mine end my purpose.

53–4. * that ... for for whom this magical music is being played.

54. staff magician's wand.

54–7. * break ... book Prospero will render his wand useless by breaking it, and inaccessible by burying it too deep for digging up, and drown his volume of magic lore in a depth of water to the bottom of which the longest plumb-line cannot reach. No one, not even he, will be able to use them again: they will be quite dead and given respectively an earthy and watery grave.

Stage Direction. **frantic gesture** perhaps the *three men of sin* enter in identical postures to those they left the stage with in Act III, Scene iii.

Stage Direction. **the circle** drawn by Prospero with his staff.

58–9. * A solemn ... brains Prospero uses the accepted theory of Renaissance times that music (harmony) is the means of soothing and settling a disturbed mind (i.e. one in a discordant state).

60. boil'd over-heated, agitated, seethed, and perhaps with the sense of reduced, liquefied, rather than hard-boiled (like an egg within its shell).

62. Holy venerable. (Though lower in rank than the three men of sin, Gonzalo is the first to be greeted.)

63–4. * Mine ... drops my eyes, full of fellow-feeling at the sight of your weeping, shed tears of sympathy.

64. apace rapidly.

65. as just as, in the same way as.

66–8. * so ... reason so their returning consciousness begins to disperse the fog of incomprehension which blankets their understanding. (Compare the truth 'dawning' on us.) The image is of early-morning mists being dissolved by the rising sun creeping over the horizon.

69. true honourable, honest.

70. him i.e. Alonso (towards whom Gonzalo's loyalty has been demonstrated during the play).

70–1. * pay ... Home reward you in full for your kindnesses.

73. * a furtherer ... act aided and abetted you in my usurpation.

74. pinch'd tormented with remorse.

74–5. * Flesh ... mine you, my brother, my own flesh and blood. The inversion of the natural order of words emphasizes the unnaturalness of Antonio's action by stressing *flesh and blood*.

75–6. * entertain'd ... nature took Ambition into your service and gave Pity and Fraternal Feeling 'the sack', (i.e. dismissed them).

75–6. * *Expell'd* is also a reminder of Antonio's expulsion of Prospero.

By my so potent art. But this rough magic   50
I here abjure; and, when I have requir'd
Some heavenly music – which even now I do –
To work mine end upon their senses that
This airy charm is for, I'll break my staff,
Bury it certain fathoms in the earth,   55
And deeper than did ever plummet sound
I'll drown my book.

       [Solemn music]

    [Here enters ARIEL before; then ALONSO, with a
    frantic gesture, attended by GONZALO; SEBASTIAN
    and ANTONIO in like manner, attended by ADRIAN
    and FRANCISCO. They all enter the circle which
    PROSPERO had made, and there stand charm'd;
    which PROSPERO observing, speaks]

A solemn air, and the best comforter
To an unsettled fancy, cure thy brains,
Now useless, boil'd within thy skull! There stand,   60
For you are spell-stopp'd.
Holy Gonzalo, honourable man,
Mine eyes, ev'n sociable to the show of thine,
Fall fellowly drops. The charm dissolves apace,
And as the morning steals upon the night,   65
Melting the darkness, so their rising senses
Begin to chase the ignorant fumes that mantle
Their clearer reason. O good Gonzalo,
My true preserver, and a loyal sir
To him thou follow'st! I will pay thy graces   70
Home both in word and deed. Most cruelly
Didst thou, Alonso, use me and my daughter;
Thy brother was a furtherer in the act.
Thou art pinch'd for't now, Sebastian. Flesh and
    blood,
You, brother mine, that entertain'd ambition,   75
Expell'd remorse and nature, who, with Sebastian –
Whose inward pinches therefore are most strong –

78. here on this island.

78. your king i.e. because Antonio has subjected the coronet of Milan to the crown of Naples (see Act I, Scene ii, line 114), Alonso is his king.

79–82. * **Their ... muddy** their minds are at present like an estuary at low tide, empty, dead, mud-bound, and useless for navigation (i.e. for receiving or conveying ideas); as consciousness returns, it is like the sea flooding back until the mud-flats are covered and the estuary is once more navigable. (The seafaring image is appropriate to the play, and adds the suggestion of happy ending with a vessel returning to port on the flood-tide.)

83. * **That yet ... know me** can see me yet, or would recognize me if he could.

85. discase me divest myself (of my magic robes).

86. * **As I ... Milan** as I used to look when I was formerly Duke of Milan.

88–94. * **Where ... bough** as he helps to transform Prospero, Ariel sings of his freedom. The setting, with its *bee, cowslip, owls, bat,* and *blossom,* is that of an English summer's day and night, rather than a Mediterranean one.

91–2. fly after follow, pursue.

96. So, so, so yes, that's it, fine! Prospero makes the final adjustments to his dress, with Ariel's help.

101. presently at once.

102. * **I drink ... before me** I suck in the air in front of me (as I fly along). Ariel moves in all the elements, but as a spirit of air he lives by that element: i.e. air is 'meat and drink' to him.

106. Sir King perhaps spoken with irony.

Would here have kill'd your king, I do forgive thee,
Unnatural though thou art. Their understanding
Begins to swell, and the approaching tide   80
Will shortly fill the reasonable shore
That now lies foul and muddy. Not one of them
That yet looks on me, or would know me. Ariel,
Fetch me the hat and rapier in my cell;
I will discase me, and myself present   85
As I was sometime Milan. Quickly, spirit;
Thou shalt ere long be free.

[ARIEL, on returning, sings and helps to attire him]

      Where the bee sucks, there suck I;
      In a cowslip's bell I lie;
      There I couch when owls do cry.   90
      On the bat's back I do fly
      After summer merrily.
    Merrily, merrily shall I live now
    Under the blossom that hangs on the bough.

Prospero
Why, that's my dainty Ariel! I shall miss thee;   95
But yet thou shalt have freedom. So, so, so.
To the King's ship, invisible as thou art;
There shalt thou find the mariners asleep
Under the hatches; the master and the boatswain
Being awake, enforce them to this place;   100
And presently, I prithee.

Ariel
I drink the air before me, and return
Or ere your pulse twice beat.

[Exit]

Gonzalo
All torment, trouble, wonder and amazement,
Inhabits here. Some heavenly power guide us   105
Out of this fearful country!

108–9. * **For … body** to reassure you that I am a living prince speaking to you (and not a spirit in disguise), I embrace you physically (so that you can feel that I am flesh and blood).

112–13. * **some … been** some magic illusion to deceive me, as I have been deceived recently (i.e. by the banquet).

115. * **Th' affliction … amends** my mind begins to recover from the affliction.

116–17. * **This … story** if all this is real and I'm not just dreaming it, then it demands a most unusual explanation.

118. * **Thy … resign** I release your Dukedom from any obligation to pay tribute to me.

119. wrongs injuries done to you (compare line 25).

120. noble friend Gonzalo.

121. embrace thine age embrace you, old man (venerable greybeard).

122. confined set limits to (i.e. because it is 'boundless').

123–4. * **You do … isle** you are still experiencing some of the illusions peculiar to the island. (The banquet in Act III, Scene iii may be alluded to in *taste … subtleties*. *Subtleties* was a term used for skilfully ornamented confections made of sugar and jelly and eaten at feasts.)

125. things certain things to be real.

126. brace pretty pair (ironically contemptuous).

126. minded disposed, inclined.

127. pluck draw, bring down.

128. justify prove (i.e. *traitors* because of their treasonous plot to kill Alonso).

129. * **The devil … him** i.e. he is a sorcerer, using black magic and being used by the devil as a mouthpiece.

129. No Prospero overhears the remark and refutes it.

131. even infect indeed contaminate.

132. rankest grossest and foulest. (The word is often used of weeds in Shakespeare, and suggests both size and smell.)

132. require demand, request (compare line 51).

Prospero   Behold, Sir King,
　The wronged Duke of Milan, Prospero.
　For more assurance that a living prince
　Does now speak to thee, I embrace thy body;
　And to thee and thy company I bid   110
　A hearty welcome.
Alonso   Whe'er thou be'st he or no,
　Or some enchanted trifle to abuse me,
　As late I have been, I not know. Thy pulse
　Beats, as of flesh and blood; and, since I saw thee,
　Th' affliction of my mind amends, with which,   115
　I fear, a madness held me. This must crave –
　An if this be at all – a most strange story.
　Thy dukedom I resign, and do entreat
　Thou pardon me my wrongs. But how should
　　　Prospero
　Be living and be here?
Prospero   First, noble friend,   120
　Let me embrace thine age, whose honour cannot
　Be measur'd or confin'd.
Gonzalo   Whether this be
　Or be not, I'll not swear.
Prospero   You do yet taste
　Some subtleties o' th' isle, that will not let you
　Believe things certain. Welcome, my friends all!   125
　[Aside to SEBASTIAN and ANTONIO] But you, my
　brace of lords, were I so minded,
　I here could pluck his Highness' frown upon you,
　And justify you traitors; at this time
　I will tell no tales.
Sebastian [Aside]
　　　　　　　The devil speaks in him.
Prospero   No.
　For you, most wicked sir, whom to call brother   130
　Would even infect my mouth, I do forgive
　Thy rankest fault – all of them; and require
　My dukedom of thee, which perforce I know

134. restore return to me.

135. * particulars ... preservation details of how you managed to survive.
136. whom who.

138. sharp the point i.e. like a knife in his heart. (Compare the phrase 'prick your conscience'.)

139. woe sorry.
140. patience the personification perhaps suggests the puritan girl's name. (Compare *Temperance*, Act II, Scene i, line 42.) Alonso's sickness of spirits is beyond the skill of Mistress Patience to cure.
142–4. * of whose ... content through whose gentle help (mercy) as nurse, I myself have her supreme power (to heal) in a similar condition (bereavement), and remain content (to accept the loss because she has soothed me with her nursing).

144. the like the same.
145. * As great ... late as heavy a loss as it is a recent one. (The economy of the language, with the added compactness of the rhyme *great ... late*, is notable.)
145–7. * supportable ... you I have much weaker resources to make bearable the loss of a dearly-loved one than you can call upon to console you (i.e. Alonso still has Claribel, but there may also be the suggestion that a daughter is more precious to a father than a son, even).
149–50. * O heavens ... there! Alonso invokes the gods to perform a miracle (which would entail his willing resignation of the crown), and it is this that Prospero has hoped to hear him say.
151. * Myself ... bed Alonso would willingly be buried/drowned if Ferdinand could only thereby be resurrected. The idea of new life springing from the dead, young king from old, is an ancient and natural one, here strongly supported in suggestion by *oozy bed*, suggesting fertility.
153. last late, recent.
154. admire wonder, marvel.
154. encounter meeting (perhaps with the suggestion of two opposed forces or champions).
155. devour their reason i.e. stand open-mouthed and uncomprehending (literally, consume their powers of reason).
155–6. * scarce ... truth they can hardly believe their eyes (i.e. that their eyes are not deceiving them, like servants who do not carry out their duties *offices* – honestly – *of truth*).
157. natural breath words spoken by human beings.
158. justled jostled, shoved, (compare Act III, Scene ii, line 25).
159. very very same, veritable.
162. yet for now.

Thou must restore.

Alonso   If thou beest Prospero,
Give us particulars of thy preservation;   135
How thou hast met us here, whom three hours since
Were wreck'd upon this shore; where I have lost –
How sharp the point of this remembrance is! –
My dear son Ferdinand.

Prospero   I am woe for't, sir.

Alonso
Irreparable is the loss; and patience   140
Says it is past her cure.

Prospero   I rather think
You have not sought her help, of whose soft grace
For the like loss I have her sovereign aid,
And rest myself content.

Alonso   You the like loss!

Prospero
As great to me as late; and, supportable   145
To make the dear loss, have I means much weaker
Than you may call to comfort you, for I
Have lost my daughter.

Alonso   A daughter!
O heavens, that they were living both in Naples,
The King and Queen there! That they were, I wish   150
Myself were mudded in that oozy bed
Where my son lies. When did you lose your daughter?

Prospero
In this last tempest. I perceive these lords
At this encounter do so much admire
That they devour their reason, and scarce think   155
Their eyes do offices of truth, their words
Are natural breath; but, howsoe'er you have
Been justled from your senses, know for certain
That I am Prospero, and that very duke
Which was thrust forth of Milan; who most strangely   160
Upon this shore, where you were wreck'd, was landed
To be the lord on't. No more yet of this;

163. * **chronicle ... day** a long story which will need several days (to tell).
164. * **relation ... breakfast** a story that can be related at a single sitting ('over the breakfast coffee').
165. Befitting suitable for.
167. abroad beyond myself. (Or he may mean around and about, beyond the immediate vicinity of his cell.)

169. requite repay.
170. bring forth a wonder produce a miracle. The re-birth of the 'lost' children is suggested by *bring forth*. In *a wonder* the miracle that both children are alive is expressed, and Miranda's name again suggested.

Stage Direction. **discovers** reveals (by drawing back the curtains of the inner stage).

Stage Direction. **playing at chess** (a) they are engaged in an aristocratic game, suitable for romantic royal lovers to play, (b) in playing chess they would be together, yet suitably separated and innocently employed.

174–5. * **Yes, for ... play** this is much disputed by editors. The meaning may be as follows: Miranda says that Ferdinand would certainly cheat her (*play me false*) if the whole world were at stake, and would even argue (*wrangle*) with her over a mere twenty kingdoms, yet in spite of this behaviour she is so much in love with him that she would still say that he was playing fairly.
176. vision illusion (i.e. which will disappear like the banquet in Act III, Scene iii).
177. * **A ... miracle** i.e. a supreme example of miraculous power (raising Ferdinand from the dead). Sebastian's astonishment seems greater than his resentment at Ferdinand's reappearance.
178. threaten look threatening.

180. compass enfold, encircle (perhaps indicating that Alonso is embracing his son, who is kneeling before him after coming forward from the cell).
181. O, wonder! it is Miranda's turn to express wonder and, herself a revelation to the courtiers, to marvel at this revelation of a new world.
182–4. * **How many ... in't** Miranda's words are unintentionally ironical if (as they seem to be) Sebastian and Antonio are unregenerate. If they *have* changed their natures, then it really is a fine (*brave*) new world, though in her present starry-eyed state it is *brave* anyway.
184. 'Tis new to thee Prospero is only being lightly ironical. He knows that the world is less *brave* than Miranda thinks (a bad old world, in fact), but there is a loving gentleness towards her wonder in his words, too.

For 'tis a chronicle of day by day,
Not a relation for a breakfast, nor
Befitting this first meeting. Welcome, sir;   165
This cell's my court; here have I few attendants,
And subjects none abroad; pray you, look in.
My dukedom since you have given me again,
I will requite you with as good a thing;
At least bring forth a wonder, to content ye   170
As much as me my dukedom.

[Here PROSPERO discovers FERDINAND and MIRANDA
               playing at chess]

Miranda
  Sweet lord, you play me false.
Ferdinand   No, my dearest love,
  I would not for the world.
Miranda
  Yes, for a score of kingdoms you should wrangle,
  And I would call it fair play.
Alonso   If this prove   175
  A vision of the island, one dear son
  Shall I twice lose.
Sebastian   A most high miracle!
Ferdinand
  Though the seas threaten, they are merciful;
  I have curs'd them without cause.

               [Kneels]

Alonso   Now all the blessings
  Of a glad father compass thee about!   180
  Arise, and say how thou cam'st here.
Miranda   O, wonder!
  How many goodly creatures are there here!
  How beauteous mankind is! O brave new world
  That has such people in't!
Prospero   'Tis new to thee.

186. * **Your … hours** you cannot have been acquainted for more than three hours.

186. three hours compare lines 136 and 223.

188–9. * **Is she … together?** Alonso's reaction to Miranda as *maid* and *goddess* is the same as his son's (compare Act I, Scene ii, lines 421 and 427). It is possible to interpret his words as a general truth: his son has been *sever'd* from him by a girl. In marrying her Ferdinand must leave his father to become 'one flesh' with his wife (i.e. the opposite of being severed), but the girl, as daughter-in-law, will be the means of reconciling father and son, perhaps more deeply uniting them than before.

188–9. * **mortal … immortal** i.e. Miranda is a mortal maid, Providence the immortal goddess.

191. advice considered opinion (and presumably his backing).

193. * **Of whom … renown** of whose high reputation I have heard so often.

196. I am hers I am (now) her father (in that Prospero is now yours).

198. my child i.e. Miranda (now his child, whose forgiveness he must ask for wronging her father).

200. heaviness sorrow (compare *heaviness may endure for a night, but joy cometh in the morning, Psalms, XXX.5*).

200. inly wept i.e. Gonzalo's heart has been too full (with tears of joy) for him to speak. (Perhaps he feels that he should, as part of his job and in civilized behaviour, *have spoke ere this*, and needs to offer an explanation of his uncharacteristic speechlessness.)

202. crown a single crown, uniting Naples and Milan. ('Holy Gonzalo', loyal to Naples and Milan, is suitably the central priest-figure at this point.)

203. chalk'd forth marked out (with chalk-marks at points along the road?). Shakespeare's only other use of 'chalk' as a verb is in *Henry VIII*, Act I, Scene i, line 60: *whose grace chalks successors their way*.

204. Amen so be it. Alonso assents to Gonzalo's prayer.

205–6. * **Milan … Naples?** Prospero turned out of his dukedom in order that (to ensure that) his descendants should become Kings of Naples?

207. common ordinary, commonplace.

207. set it down inscribe it.

208. lasting perhaps with a suggestion of 'everlasting'.

208. one a single.

209. find meet (in the sense of 'finding a husband'?), or perhaps 'found him waiting'.

211. Prospero his dukedom i.e. found his dukedom.

212. and all of us ourselves i.e. found ourselves (the truth about ourselves).

213. own i.e. himself (in control of himself).

Alonso
  What is this maid with whom thou wast at play?   185
  Your eld'st acquaintance cannot be three hours;
  Is she the goddess that hath sever'd us,
  And brought us thus together?
Ferdinand   Sir, she is mortal;
  But by immortal Providence she's mine.
  I chose her when I could not ask my father   190
  For his advice, nor thought I had one. She
  Is daughter to this famous Duke of Milan,
  Of whom so often I have heard renown
  But never saw before; of whom I have
  Receiv'd a second life; and second father   195
  This lady makes him to me.
Alonso   I am hers.
  But, O, how oddly will it sound that I
  Must ask my child forgiveness!
Prospero   There, sir, stop;
  Let us not burden our remembrances with
  A heaviness that's gone.
Gonzalo   I have inly wept,   200
  Or should have spoke ere this. Look down, you
      gods,
  And on this couple drop a blessed crown;
  For it is you that have chalk'd forth the way
  Which brought us hither.
Alonso   I say, Amen, Gonzalo!
Gonzalo
  Was Milan thrust from Milan, that his issue   205
  Should become Kings of Naples? O, rejoice
  Beyond a common joy, and set it down
  With gold on lasting pillars: in one voyage
  Did Claribel her husband find at Tunis;
  And Ferdinand, her brother, found a wife   210
  Where he himself was lost; Prospero his dukedom
  In a poor isle; and all of us ourselves
  When no man was his own.

205–13. * Gonzalo's speech summarizes the story of the main events with impressive economy. It is in a sense 'the last word' and all that remains is for the characters to come down to earth again with the arrival of the comic characters, Boatswain and comic trio.

213. Give me your hands Alonso echoes Prospero's action of Act IV, Scene i.

214–15. * **Let … joy** may grief and sorrow for ever possess (grip) the heart of anyone who does not join me in wishing you every happiness. (Prospero has embraced Alonso, and then Gonzalo; Alonso has embraced Ferdinand, and perhaps Miranda at line 196, *I am hers*. Their embracing has been a loving and happy action. The only embracing received by the hard-hearted, e.g. Sebastian and Antonio, is given by unhappiness.)

Stage Direction. **amazedly** in a bewildered state.

218. blasphemy you blasphemous fellow.

219. * **swear'st … overboard** i.e. by swearing, removes God's grace (divine protection) from the ship.

221. best news i.e. that we are talking with you now.

223. * **Which … spilt** which only three hours ago we said had gone on the rocks (was wrecked).

224. tight and yare ship-shape, trim and ready.

226. tricksy ingenious, clever.

227–8. * **strengthen … stranger** grow stranger and stranger (to listen to).

230. of sleep asleep. (The resurrection image is reinforced by *dead:* the mariners have also been roused and raised from a metaphorical death.)

231. * **clapp'd … hatches** i.e. imprisoned below deck (compare the phrase 'clapped in irons').

232. but even now only a moment ago.

232. several separate, distinct. (Compare Act III, Scene i, line 42.)

235. We were awak'd i.e. we were woken up by the *strange and several noises*. The inverted construction puts the actions in their right sequence: first, the noises, then the waking up. (The noises seem to be those of prisoners in chains: the mariners have not been in irons, but their release from below the hatches would seem as if they had been.)

236. in all her trim compare *tight and yare* in line 224. The ship was spick and span, and ready to sail. (Like the garments of the nobles, the vessel seems fresher than before.)

236. Freshly once more, afresh (though there is also the sense of the ship being beheld freshly rigged out).

237. * **royal … gallant** i.e. royal (because carrying the king), good (because sound), and gallant (because fine, 'brave'). 'Royal' and 'gallant' are also used to describe certain masts and sails: the Boatswain is not simply describing the ship's qualities but also her appearance.

237–8. * **our master … her** 'Our Captain jumping for joy at seeing her (in such good shape).' The Master would no doubt have been confined to his cabin and so separated from his crew as suited his position, otherwise he would presumably have told the story. (Also his part being one for a minor actor in Act I, Scene i, and the Boatswain's for an actor of some power, the Master would be less suitable to give the graphic account, and in fact is given nothing to say!)

Alonso [To FERDINAND and MIRANDA]
                              Give me your hands.
  Let grief and sorrow still embrace his heart
  That doth not wish you joy.
Gonzalo   Be it so. Amen!   215

  [Re-enter ARIEL, with the MASTER and BOATSWAIN
          amazedly following]

  O look, sir; look, sir! Here is more of us!
  I prophesied, if a gallows were on land,
  This fellow could not drown. Now, blasphemy,
  That swear'st grace o'erboard, not an oath on
      shore?
  Hast thou no mouth by land? What is the news?   220
Boatswain
  The best news is that we have safely found
  Our King and company; the next, our ship –
  Which but three glasses since we gave out split –
  Is tight and yare, and bravely rigg'd, as when
  We first put out to sea.
Ariel [Aside to Prospero.]
                          Sir, all this service   225
  Have I done since I went.
Prospero [Aside to ARIEL]
                          My tricksy spirit!
Alonso
  These are not natural events; they strengthen
  From strange to stranger. Say, how came you hither?
Boatswain
  If I did think, sir, I were well awake,
  I'd strive to tell you. We were dead of sleep,   230
  And – how, we know not – all clapp'd under hatches;
  Where, but even now, with strange and several noises
  Of roaring, shrieking, howling, jingling chains,
  And more diversity of sounds, all horrible,
  We were awak'd; straightway at liberty;   235
  Where we, in all her trim, freshly beheld
  Our royal, good, and gallant ship; our master

237–8. on a trice in a flash, suddenly.

239. we i.e. Master and Boatswain.

239. them i.e. the ship's crew.

240. moping in befuddled, bewildered fashion (with suggestions of sulkiness and being downcast).

241. * Bravely … diligence splendidly, my punctilious and efficient one.

242. * maze … trod see note to Act III, Scene iii, line 2. The image is that of trying to reach the truth along the tortuous paths of life's labyrinthine journey with its unexpected and baffling twists and turns.

244. conduct conductor, guide.

245. my liege although Alonso has resigned Milan to Prospero (line 118), as a king he is still senior to him and is therefore courteously addressed as *liege*, sovereign lord.

246. infest trouble, agitate.

246. beating on 'hammering away at (in your mind).' Compare Act I, Scene ii, line 176 and Act IV, Scene i, line 163. (And also compare *King Lear*, Act III, Scene iv, line 14: *The tempest in my mind Doth from my senses take all feeling else Save what beats there.*)

247–50. * at pick'd … accidents at a suitable opportunity in the near future, I'll give you an explanation in private, and show it to be perfectly capable of proof, of each of the events which have just taken place.

251. well as being for the best.

253. * How … sir? how are you getting on, my noble lord? Alonso is still bemused, and Prospero speaks to him as a doctor might to a patient 'coming round'.

255. odd extra.

256–7. * Every … fortune perhaps Stephano is trying to show leadership by saying that they must all work together in spite of any setbacks, though it sounds more as though he has unwittingly muddled his sentences and intended to say, 'Every man shift for himself …'.

257–8. Coragio, bully-monster cheer up, my fine monster, take heart.

259. true spies truthful eyes, (literally, spies who bring an accurate report of what they have seen).

Cap'ring to eye her. On a trice, so please you,
Even in a dream, were we divided from them,
And were brought moping hither.
Ariel [Aside to PROSPERO]
       Was't well done?   240
Prospero [Aside to ARIEL]
Bravely, my diligence. Thou shalt be free.
Alonso
This is as strange a maze as e'er men trod;
And there is in this business more than nature
Was ever conduct of. Some oracle
Must rectify our knowledge.
Prospero   Sir, my liege,   245
Do not infest your mind with beating on
The strangeness of this business; at pick'd leisure,
Which shall be shortly, single I'll resolve you,
Which to you shall seem probable, of every
These happen'd accidents; till when, be cheerful 250
And think of each thing well. [Aside to ARIEL]
   Come hither, spirit;
Set Caliban and his companions free;
Untie the spell.

     [Exit ARIEL]

   How fares my gracious sir?
There are yet missing of your company
Some few odd lads that you remember not.   255

[Re-enter ARIEL, driving in CALIBAN, STEPHANO, and
  TRINCULO, in their stolen apparel]

Stephano
Every man shift for all the rest, and let no man take
care for himself; for all is but fortune. Coragio,
bully-monster, coragio!
Trinculo
If these be true spies which I wear in my head,
here's a goodly sight.   260

261. O Setebos Caliban swears by his *dam's god* (see Act I, Scene ii, line 373).

261. brave spirits Caliban's exclamation echoes Miranda's in line 182.

262. * How fine ... is i.e. dressed as Duke of Milan.

265–6. * Will ... marketable Sebastian and Antonio treat Caliban (and less seriously, Stephano and Trinculo) as mere things from which to make a profit at a fair, and thus precisely parallel Stephano and Trinculo's first reactions to Caliban.

265–6. plain fish clearly a fish (presumably from the smell: see note to Act II, Scene ii, line 26).

267. * Mark ... badges just look at the livery coat-of-arms. Prospero is either drawing attention to the royal arms of Naples on Stephano's and Trinculo's own clothing or to the ducal arms of Milan on their stolen garments. In either case they are not *true* (i.e. honest) men because they are wearing stolen garments. (There could also be an implicit reference to Antonio, who metaphorically put on the livery of Naples over that of Milan.) *Badges* may, however, mean simply the stolen garments.

268. This as for this.

270. That that she.

271. * dead ... power exercise the authority of the moon but independently of the moon itself, (i.e. she received her power from her witchcraft and not from the moon).

272–3. * demi-devil ... bastard i.e. neither pure devil nor purely human but the product of the Devil and a witch. See Act I, Scene ii, line 319.

275. thing of darkness (a) Caliban, born of evil, (b) Caliban, dark-skinned. (Prospero may also be referring to Caliban as the dark, animal side or part of his own nature as a human being, with Miranda and/or Ariel perhaps symbolizing his fair, spiritual side.)

279. reeling ripe staggering drunkenly (full of wine).

280. grand liquor potent brew.

280. gilded flushed their faces (i.e. they were 'all lit up').

282. pickle state, mess (a) from their soaking in the pond, (b) because drunk, (c) because caught thieving.

283. pickle Trinculo, professional jester, can still manage a weak pun: *pickle* now becomes the wine (vinegar) in which his body is saturated, steeped.

283–4. * I ... fly-blowing i.e. because his body is 'meat' preserved in pickling alcohol, and flies will therefore not contaminate it (only laying their eggs in fresh or decomposing flesh).

286. * Stephano ... cramp one great cramp, aching all over.

Caliban
    O Setebos, these be brave spirits indeed!
    How fine my master is! I am afraid
    He will chastise me.
Sebastian   Ha, ha!
    What things are these, my lord Antonio?
    Will money buy 'em?
Antonio   Very like; one of them   265
    Is a plain fish, and no doubt marketable.
Prospero
    Mark but the badges of these men, my lords,
    Then say if they be true. This mis-shapen knave –
    His mother was a witch, and one so strong
    That could control the moon, make flows and ebbs,   270
    And deal in her command without her power.
    These three have robb'd me; and this demi-devil –
    For he's a bastard one – had plotted with them
    To take my life. Two of these fellows you
    Must know and own; this thing of darkness I   275
    Acknowledge mine.
Caliban   I shall be pinch'd to death.
Alonso
    Is not this Stephano, my drunken butler?
Sebastian
    He is drunk now; where had he wine?
Alonso
    And Trinculo is reeling ripe; where should they
    Find this grand liquor that hath gilded 'em?   280
    How cam'st thou in this pickle?
Trinculo
    I have been in such a pickle since I saw you last
    that, I fear me, will never out of my bones. I shall
    not fear flyblowing.   285
Sebastian
    Why, how now, Stephano!

288. a sore one probably further punning, i.e. (a) aching, (b) sorry, (c) strict.

290. * disproportion'd ... manners ugly in his behaviour.

292. look hope, expect.

295. grace pardon, mercy.
295. thrice-double probably of no particular significance as an epithet, but Shakespeare uses the prefix 'thrice' quite often, usually in praising. There are four instances in his plays of 'thrice-noble', and *thrice-double ass* could be the antithesis of 'thrice-noble lord'. (Perhaps *ass* because an ass carried the drunken Silenus about, who though not a god himself was foster-father to a god, Bacchus, god of wine.)
297. worship respect, honour, reverence.
297. dull fool stupid idiot, (i.e. Alonso's Fool or Jester should have been sharp-witted, whereas Trinculo has been duped).
297. go to that's enough, get on with it.
298. luggage see note to Act IV, Scene i, line 231.

300. train retinue, followers.

302. waste spend, use up.

305. accidents events.

307. bring escort, accompany, conduct.

Stephano
  O, touch me not; I am not Stephano, but a cramp.
Prospero
  You'd be king 'o the isle, sirrah?
Stephano
  I should have been a sore one, then.
Alonso [Pointing to CALIBAN]
  This is as strange a thing as e'er I look'd on.
Prospero
  He is as disproportion'd in his manners   290
  As in his shape. Go, sirrah, to my cell;
  Take with you your companions; as you look
  To have my pardon, trim it handsomely.
Caliban
  Ay, that I will; and I'll be wise hereafter,
  And seek for grace. What a thrice-double ass   295
  Was I to take this drunkard for a god,
  And worship this dull fool!
Prospero   Go to; away!
Alonso
  Hence, and bestow your luggage where you found
      it.
Sebastian
  Or stole it, rather.

    [Exeunt CALIBAN, STEPHANO, and TRINCULO]

Prospero
  Sir, I invite your Highness and your train   300
  To my poor cell, where you shall take your rest
  For this one night; which, part of it, I'll waste
  With such discourse as, I not doubt, shall make it
  Go quick away – the story of my life,
  And the particular accidents gone by   305
  Since I came to this isle. And in the morn
  I'll bring you to your ship, and so to Naples,
  Where I have hope to see the nuptial
  Of these our dear-belov'd solemnized,
  And thence retire me to my Milan, where   310

311. * **Every ... grave** perhaps connected with Act IV, Scene i, line 3, in which case one thought is for Miranda, one for Milan, and one for his own approaching end.

313. * **Take ... strangely** strike one as something very unusual, rare.
313. deliver all tell it in detail.
314. auspicious gales favourable (i.e. following) winds.
315–16. * **And sail ... far off** and such speedy sailing that you will soon overtake the rest of your royal fleet, which is already well on its way.

318. * **Please ... near** please go in (to the cell). As the actors enter the cell, Prospero is left alone on the stage to speak his farewell to the audience.

Every third thought shall be my grave.
Alonso
                                        I long
To hear the story of your life, which must
Take the ear strangely.
Prospero   I'll deliver all;
And promise you calm seas, auspicious gales,
And sail so expeditious that shall catch   315
Your royal fleet far off. [Aside to Ariel] My Ariel,
        chick,
That is thy charge. Then to the elements
Be free, and fare thou well! – Please you, draw near.

[Exeunt]

EPILOGUE

1. Now ... o'erthrown now all my spells have been discarded.

3. faint weak, feeble.
4. confin'd kept here.

6. got got back.
7. the deceiver i.e. Antonio.
8. bare empty, uninhabited (Prospero gesturing towards the empty stage around him, perhaps).
9. bands bonds. Prospero, who has been binding and releasing throughout the play, now begs for his own freedom.
10. * with ... hands (a) by undoing or untying the *bands* with which he is bound, (b) releasing him by clapping their hands in applause.
11. Gentle breath kind remarks, favourable comments (like the *auspicious gales* of Act V, Scene i, line 314) on the play.
12. project purpose (compare Act V, Scene i, line 1).
13. want both meanings, wish or desire *and* lack or need, are present: i.e. Prospero desires Ariel and his spirits to force the audience to grant his release by magic spells, but he himself lacks spirits or magic to do so.
15. despair dejection, abandoning hope (compare *desperation*, suicidal thoughts, in Act I, Scene ii, line 210, and *desperate*, suicidal, in Act III, Scene iii, line 104).
16. reliev'd raised up again, restored.
16. by prayer (a) by my requests to you, or (b) by your intercessions for me.
17–18. * Which ... faults a plea which is so piercing that it reaches to the Mercy-seat of God the Judge and persuades Him to forgive all shortcomings and to give them a free pardon. (The playwright throws himself on the mercy of the audience, who are judging the play.)
19. * would ... be wish to be pardoned.
20. indulgence lenient attitude. (A Papal indulgence was a pardon remitting temporal punishment still due for sins whose eternal punishment has been sacramentally absolved.)

EPILOGUE

Now my charms are all o'erthrown,
And what strength I have's mine own,
Which is most faint. Now 'tis true,
I must be here confin'd by you,
Or sent to Naples. Let me not,   5
Since I have my dukedom got,
And pardon'd the deceiver, dwell
In this bare island by your spell;
But release me from my bands
With the help of your good hands.   10
Gentle breath of yours my sails
Must fill, or else my project fails,
Which was to please. Now I want
Spirits to enforce, art to enchant;
And my ending is despair   15
Unless I be reliev'd by prayer,
Which pierces so that it assaults
Mercy itself, and frees all faults.
As you from crimes would pardon'd be,
Let your indulgence set me free.   20

SUMMING UP

It was suggested in the Introduction that *The Tempest* is a play in which themes are more important than characters, and that the characters are perhaps best understood if viewed as *kinds* of people rather than as particular individuals; that the play does not, because it is so short, develop its characters 'warts and all'. Assuming this to be so, any comments on the characters should be linked closely with the themes illuminated by those characters: in no Shakespeare play are themes merely incidental to the characters or characters purely there to express themes, but in *The Tempest* there is an unusually close relationship between the two.

In Prospero, for example, most of the central ideas of the play converge. The idea of *discovery* and *self-discovery* can be seen in the events before as well as on the island: while still Duke in Milan he is an explorer in the realms of his magic art who also discovers truths about human nature when his brother usurps his title, as he does on the island later when he discovers that simple Caliban is as treacherous as sophisticated Antonio. He is an idealist who is forced to become a realist. And in this 'becoming' he is an example of the theme of *change* which threads its way through the play: it is not only that he changes the lives of others, he is himself changed by the events he creates. The transformation of Prospero from someone exulting in having his enemies in his power, so that he can avenge the murderous wrongs done to him and his only child by them, to someone who becomes able to forgive them, is the principal metamorphosis in the play. The ideas that characters are tested by events is common to most plays, which are mirrors of the trials of life itself; it is more prominent in *The Tempest* because it is Prospero rather than accidental circumstances who is seen as doing the proving (for example, by testing Ferdinand) and he is himself tested crucially when he has to choose between 'virtue' or 'Vengeance' (Act V, Scene i, line 28). In choosing forgiveness rather than revenge, love rather than hate, he releases himself from bondage to the past. And here two threads lie close together. The idea of *imprisonment and release* is continually present in the play generally, and in Prospero particularly. As he shows in the agitated violence of his feelings about the events of his usurpation, which lie a long time off (Act I, Scene ii, lines 66–168), twelve years back, the past is still vividly present and real: he is still imprisoned by its memory. He spellbinds and releases characters during the play, but it is himself whom he releases in releasing them. Much of the play is about *freedom* and how Prospero and the other characters achieve it at different spiritual and physical levels. (It is rather appropriate that he should leave his *cell* at the end of the play.)

The Tempest has sometimes been criticized for lacking any true dramatic conflict, because Prospero is so powerful that he can manipulate the characters like puppets. What is often overlooked is that he cannot control their wills (boiling their brains within their skulls is equivalent to anaesthetizing them temporarily); and more important, that the conflict is within Prospero himself. He may *control* the characters physically, but it is the exercise of *self-control* that Prospero has to learn. In order to become a magician he has had to learn the art of self-discipline; it is during the play and at the most testing moment for him that he has to exercise that self-control through which he restrains himself from taking his revenge.

It is only through self-control that men can effectively or productively govern others, and Prospero shows how difficult this exercise of control is to achieve in his relationship with his two servants, Ariel and Caliban. When Ariel protests (Act I, Scene ii, lines 242–9) that Prospero has not yet released him as promised, he receives a sharp reply from his master, so anxious is Prospero not to lose him at the very moment when he is most needed. Ariel symbolizes Man's spiritual nature or his imagination, and it is possible to see Prospero as representing the artist managing the materials of his art through the control of his creative imagination. The rebellious Ariel, like the artist's imagination, is controlled and put to creative use only with difficulty, though once under control he is as joyful and rapid as the imagination working without restraint. Prospero's other servant, Caliban, is also rebellious and needs to be kept under control: he is *this thing of darkness* (Act V, Scene i, line 275) which Prospero acknowledges as his own, the animal part of human nature with its potentially destructive drives needing to be put to constructive use.

Caliban is shown as raw nature needing to be nurtured, or educated. (The play repeats the idea of educating oneself and others in a number of places.) During the play it seems that Prospero, who like all artists is a teacher, has failed to civilize him and despairs of doing so. And when Antonio and Sebastian appear to be unrepentant at the end of the play it looks as though Prospero will have to accept that there is a dark part of human personality which is incapable of reformation. Yet perhaps Caliban suggests that there is always hope even in the hardest of hard cases, when he says that he will be *wise hereafter, and seek for grace* (Act V, Scene i, lines 294–5).

Throughout the play there is a strong feeling that events are moving towards a future, and that 'hereafter' men will lead changed lives. Prospero's part is to control the present so that a fruitful future can follow. *Time* in one form or another is insistently referred to: in Prospero's looking into the past, and in his awareness of the need to seize his opportunities in the present to redeem the past and prepare the future. He can be seen as the older generation handing over hopefully to the younger. Yet though he uses Time to bring good out of evil, he recognizes that as a human being he is himself subject to *Providence divine* and to a destiny which is shaping his end also.

His marriage-masque for Miranda and Ferdinand is the best gift that he can present to them, being a wise vision of life's potentiality. A sense of *wonder* is the response of the lovers to the masque, just as it is the reaction of most of the characters to the events on the island. And although it is the impresario-figure Prospero who presents these wonders, he is capable of being surprised himself (for example, when Miranda is able to recall infant memories from *the dark backward and abysm of time*) and his daughter's name may indicate his wonder at having a daughter. In fact the capacity for being surprised and able to wonder seems to belong to all the characters except the cynical Antonio and Sebastian. The origins of the theme no doubt lie in the *Sea Adventure* source (see Introduction and the Appendix) and the feeling of miraculous escape, and lead through the stage devices used in masque-theatre to the idea that truths can suddenly be revealed to men, and often under the pressure of disorientating experiences.

Prospero is not the only character who expresses the central concerns of the play: all the characters relate to them in a variety of ways, and express other themes as well. Among these themes may be found one which Shakespeare reiterates throughout his work, the idea of *loyalty and treachery*. He juxtaposes the loyalty of the selfless Gonzalo with the treachery of the self-seeking Antonio and Sebastian, and underlines their plot against Alonso in the comic sub-plot of Caliban, Trinculo and Stephano's plan to murder Prospero. The idea of playing false can be seen in Prospero's warning to Ferdinand and Miranda to be true to their vows of chastity, and even perhaps in Miranda's gentle rebuke *My lord, you play me false* (Act V, Scene i, line 172). Even Miranda is guilty of breaking her vow inadvertently when she gives her name to Ferdinand (Act III, Scene i, line 37). All instances of disloyalty reflect Antonio's initial treachery towards Prospero, which is not only that of subject to ruler in the state but of younger to older brother in the microcosm of the state, the family.

Acts of treachery are breaches of that natural, divinely-ordered hierarchical system which was for Elizabethans the basis of society. When Gonzalo describes his ideal classless commonwealth (Act II, Scene i, lines 143–59) he is expressing not only contemporary hopes of finding and founding a brave new world on the far side of the Atlantic, but is conscious that the visionary utopia he is proposing is unlikely to replace a hierarchical society, men being what they are. The sneering cynicism of Antonio and Sebastian is exposed by their reaction to his day-dreaming; their dreams are only of personal power based upon things remaining as they are. Nevertheless, though Gonzalo is realist enough to know that his utopia is hardly a practical possibility, he also knows that men can only live by hope of a better future. As a character he is like others in *The Tempest*, both a person and a figure. On the ship he shows the fear that any human being would; on the island he becomes the embodiment of Faith, Hope and Charity. At the mock-banquet (Act III, Scene iii,) he says that Alonso should put more trust in Providence (*Faith sir, you need not fear*); he shows a more than merely diplomatic cheerfulness in contrast to Alonso's despair; and his charitable actions are gratefully referred to by Prospero in Act I, Scene ii, lines 160–8. Whether or not Shakespeare was intending to convey a specifically Christian message in *The Tempest* is probably a matter of opinion and emphasis, but much of its terminology (words like *holy, grace, mercy, blessed, pardon*) echoes New Testament language, as do themes and images of resurrection and forgiveness.

The idea of *loss* and *recovery* is also important: through loss the characters are tested and learn. Prospero learns patience through the loss of his dukedom; Alonso learns remorse through the loss of Ferdinand; in losing something precious, something more precious is found. As well as experiencing the loss of family and friends, the characters find that they have lost their way (symbolically, in life) as they tread the maze (Act III, Scene iii, line 2) of the island's paths and find no way out. The theme is summed up in Act V, Scene i, lines 205–13 when Gonzalo says that in the moment of loss they each 'found themselves', and there is an echo in his words of the Christian message that whoever loses his life shall find it.

Shakespeare's comic scenes exist partly to provide relief from the tensions of the main action and partly to reflect the main themes. In the Trinculo-Stephano sub-plot their words and actions parody and caricature much of the serious content of the play: a distorting mirror is held up and we laugh as we see the truth. Their drunken imitation of court behaviour (Act III, Scene ii, lines 1–55), their greedy plotting to seize power by murder (Act III, Scene ii, lines 56–110), their shallow preoccupation with the trappings of authority (Act IV, Scene i, lines 222–53) precisely echo the main themes of self-control, treachery and deceit. In their scale of values a bottle becomes a Bible, and when they complain (Act IV, Scene i, lines 208–10) that there is disgrace and dishonour in its loss in the pool, we are reminded of the dignity and seriousness of the upper level of the action. The way in which the comic can recall and underline the tragic is shown when Caliban says *All's hushed as midnight yet* (Act IV, Scene i, line 207) on the threshold of Prospero's cell, and we remember that *midnight fated to the purpose* (Act I, Scene ii, lines 128–9) of twelve years before.

As a trio, Caliban, Trinculo and Stephano provide an image of the turbulence and discord which contrast with the harmony created by Prospero as he imposes order on uncontrolled nature by means of reason and the development of self-discipline: they speak a blunt prose which contrasts with the musical verse of the main plot; the rough rhythms and words of their songs are the antithesis of Ariel's sweet airs; their response to his tabor and pipe is that of *unback'd colts*, wild animals.

Music is the most important element in *The Tempest*, both as stage-sound and as symbol; it is no mere ornament. Shakespeare uses it to create an ambiance in which we accept the supernatural events; Prospero uses it as the medium through which he exercises his magic; after the realistic chaos of the storm scene, which presents a picture of actual life with its dangers and disorders, music removes the action to a higher and more abstract plane of existence so that we see the characters in their essence and as representative human beings. Ferdinand and Miranda are not so much two unique and individualized personalities as the embodiment of romantic love: they are all lovers who fall in love at first sight (and have their first tiff – Act V, Scene i, line 172), whose falling in love is a wonderful discovery, and whose only wish is to serve each other faithfully. The words of their duet in Act III, Scene i are not intended to reproduce everyday conversation but to convey the harmony of their feelings, in the way that a love-song expresses the lyrical ecstasy of emotion which is part of, but transcends, sexual passion.

Caliban's unrestrained sexual appetite is that of nature run wild. Before the masque, through which he blesses

Miranda's marriage with fertility, Prospero warns Ferdinand to exercise self-control; the wanton power of Venus is thwarted and Ceres presents an image of the fruitful productiveness which results from cultivation. The device of a play-within-a-play is used on a number of occasions by Shakespeare to underline a play's main concerns by repeating them in miniature. *The Tempest* is itself a masque-like play, and Prospero's masque is a microcosm of it. The idea that the future depends upon the young – in this case Ferdinand and Miranda – to bring a brave new world into being from the bad old world of their parents is the message of the play, and when the goddesses bless the betrothal with harmony and fruitfulness they present a vision of the outcome of Prospero's plan.

If we approach *The Tempest* expecting realism in characterization, plot or setting we will be disappointed. It is too compressed a play for more than a limited development of its characters; and the characters themselves are too restricted in independence of action to achieve their aims without Prospero's manipulation. The fact that we do not experience the events in Milan at first hand – events from which the action stems – together with references to how remote the events are in time and space, helps to set the events on the island at a distance from reality. At the same time there is a concentration of language which combines with an economy of action to produce a picture of life rather than life itself. Shakespeare was exploring beyond realism in his final Romances to create plays which have the timeless poetic power of fairy-tales and myths, yet remain part of the ordinary world of particular timebound events.

APPENDIX

Extracts from William Strachey's letter dated 15 July 1610, generally referred to as the *True Reportory of the Wracke*, which was almost certainly known to Shakespeare.

... a dreadful storme and hideous began to blow from out the North-east, which swelling, and roaring as it were by fits, some houres with more violence then others, at length did beate all light from heaven; which like an hell of darknesse turned blacke upon us ... For foure and twenty houres, the storme in a restlesse tumult, had blowne to exceedingly, as we could not apprehende in our imaginations any possibility of greater violence, yet did wee still finde it, not onely more terrible, but more constant, fury added to fury, and one storme urging a second more outragious than the former ... our clamours dround in the windes, and the windes in thunder. Prayers might well be in the heart and lips, but drowned in the outcries of the Officers: nothing heard that could give comfort, nothing seene that might encourage hope ... The sea swelled above the Clouds, and gave battell unto Heaven. It could not be said to raine, the waters like whole Rivers did flood in the ayre ... the glut of water (as if throatling the winde ere while) was no sooner a little emptied and qualified, but instantly the windes (as having gotten their mouthes now free, and at liberty) spake more loud, and grew more tumultuous, and malignant ... Howbeit this was not all; it pleased God to bring a greater affliction yet upon us; for in the beginning of the storme we had received likewise a mighty leake. And the Ship in every joint almost, having spued out her Okam, before we were aware ... was growne five foote suddenly deepe with water above her ballast, and we almost drowned within, whilest we sat looking when to perish from above. ... During all this time, the heavens look'd so blacke upon us, that it was not possible the elevation of the Pole might be observed: nor a Starre by night, nor Sunne beame by day was to be seene. Onely upon the Thursday night Sir George Summers being upon the watch, had an apparition of a little round light, like a faint Starre, trembling, and streaming along with a sparkling blaze, halfe the height upon the Maine Mast, and shooting sometimes from Shroud to Shroud, tempting to settle as it were upon any of the foure Shrouds: and for three or foure houres together, or rather more, halfe the night it kept with us; running sometimes along the Maine-yard to the very end, and then returning ... we steered away as much as we could to beare upright ... we much unrigged our Ship, threw overboard much luggage, many a Trunke and Chest ... and staved many a Butt of Beere, Hogsheads of Oyle, Syder, Wine, and Vinegar ... But see the goodnesse and sweet introduction of better hope, by our merciful God given unto us. Sir George Summers, when no man dreamed of such happinesse, had discovered, and cried Land ... We were inforced to runne her ashoare, as neere the land as we could, which brought us within three quarters of a mile of shoare ...

We found it to be the dangerous and dreaded Iland, or rather Ilands of the Bermuda ... so terrible to all that ever touched on them, and such tempests, thunders, and other fearfull objects are seen and heard about them, that they be called commonly, The Devils Ilands, and are feared and avoyded of all sea travellers alive, above any other place in the world. Yet it pleased our merciful God, to make even this hideous and hated place, both the place of our safetie, and meanes of our deliverance.

And hereby also, I hope to deliver the world from a foule and general error: it being counted of most, that they can be no habitation for Men, but rather given over to Devils, and wicked Spirits; whereas indeed wee find them now by experience, to bee as habitable and commodious as most Countries of the same climate and situation: ... Thus we shall make it appeare, That Truth is the daughter of Time, and that men ought not to deny every thing which is not subject to their owne sense ...

[Strachey then mentions that there was a lack of rivers and *running Springs of fresh water*, but a ready supply of seamew-sized sea-birds which were attracted by the sailors *hollowing, laughing, and making the strangest outcry,* in response to which the birds came *answering the noise themselves* and tamely allowed themselves to be taken. He also mentions the *Tortoyse* as being *such a kind of meat as man can neither absolutely call Fish or Flesh* ... After which he describes mutinies among the survivors of the shipwreck.]

In these dangers and divellish disquiets (whilest the almighty God wrought for us, and sent us miraculously delivered from the calamities of the Sea, all blessings upon the shoare, to content and binde us to gratefulnesse) thus inraged amongst our selves, to the destruction each of other, into what a mischiefe and misery had wee bin given up, had wee not had a Governour with his authority, to have suppressed the same? ...

But as all giddy and lawlesse attempts, have alwayes something of imperfection, and that as well by the property of the action, which holdeth of disobedience and rebellion (both full of feare) as through the ignorance of the devisers themselves; so in this (besides those defects) there were some of the association, who not strong inough fortified in their own conceits, brake from the plot it selfe; and (before the time was ripe for the execution thereof) discovered the whole order, and every Agent, and Actor thereof, who neverthelesse were not suddenly apprehended, by reason the confederates were divided and seperated in place, some with us, and the chiefe with Sir George Summers in his Iland (and indeed all his whole company) but good watch passed upon them, every man from thence forth commanded to weare his weapon ... and advised to stand upon his guard, his owne life not being in safety whilest his next neighbour was not to be trusted.

NOTES TO APPENDIX

If Shakespeare's imagination was in fact excited by Strachey's account, we may see the origin of several ideas and even phrases in it, some of which are listed below:
the violence of the storm
roaring: Act I, Scene i, line 16, *hell of darkness* Act I, Scene ii,

line 214; *sea swelled ... gave battle* Act I, Scene ii, lines 3–5; *glut of water* Act I, Scene i, line 59; *free ... liberty ... malignant* Act I, Scene ii, lines 245 and 257; *heavens ... black* Act I, Scene ii, line 3.

the condition of the vessel
leak: Act I, Scene i, line 46.

electricity
an apparition ... then returning: Act I, Scene ii, lines 196–201

the management of the vessel
steered away ... upright: Act I, Scene i, lines 48–9, *unrigged our ship:* Act I, Scene i, line 33.

jettisoning of stores
threw overboard ... vinegar: Act II, Scene ii, line 118.

Bermudas called 'The Devil's Ilands'
all the devils are here: Act I, Scene ii, line 215; *Bermoothes:* Act I, Scene ii, line 229.

climate
habitable ... situation: Act II, Scene i, lines 34–51.

Truth is the daughter of Time
a central idea of the play, that the truth will be revealed in due course.

Tortoyse ... Fish or Flesh
Act I, Scene ii, line 316; Act II, Scene ii, lines 24–6.

miraculous delivery
miraculous ... calamities ... gratefulness: Act II, Scene i, lines 1–9.

plotting and divisions
Governor with his authority is perhaps a Prospero-figure, *divided and separated:* Act I, Scene ii, line 220; *watch ... weapon ... guard:* Act II, Scene ii, lines 317–18.

THEME INDEX

The central theme in the play is that of *metamorphosis* or *change*; many of the transformations are produced within the characters by the external action of Prospero's magic. Closely associated with change is the key word *strange*.

Change:

I ii 66–109 (in Antonio); Ariel's various costume changes; I ii 401–2; the sudden end of the Masque in IV; IV i 148–56; IV i 246–8; Prospero changes heart V i 20–30, and costume V i 85–6.

Prospero's magic works through music, which represents order, the sweet music of Ariel's songs, the harsh music of thunder, the stirring music of tabor and pipe. Comic songs contrast with the solemn and supernatural airs.

Music:

I ii 375–405; II i 177 and 292–301; II ii 41–55, 173–80; III ii 116–48; III iii 18, 82, 97–9; IV i 59, 106–17, 175–8; V i 58, 88–94.

It is in human relationships that order and disorder, loyalty and treachery, are most fully displayed in this as in all Shakespeare's plays, on the political, social, family or personal level.

Relationships:

I i (throughout); I ii 56–9, 66–77, 118–22; Prospero with Ariel, I ii 250–300, and throughout the play; with Caliban, I ii 344–74, and throughout the play; II i 67–8, 143–59, 251–70; II ii 68–78; the whole of III i; the comic dissensions in III ii; IV i 14–22; V i 20–31, 71–9, 137–52, 190–9, 209–14.

Love and forgiveness set free, hatred and revenge imprison. The idea of *bondage* and *release* is expressed throughout the play.

Bondage and Release:

I ii 185–6, 230–2, 250–96, 326, 342–3, 360–2, 461, 486–94; II ii 181–2; III i 4–15, 41, 89; III iii 2 (the maze as prison), 88–90; IV i 120–2, 181–2, 263–5; V i 7–11, 30–2, 41–57,

58–68, 79–82, 231–6, 252–3, 319–20, Epilogue 4–10, 19–20. Sleep is a sort of bondage yet asleep we can escape in our dreams.

Sleep and Dreams:
I ii 45, 185–6, 486; II i 181–96, 205–12, 296–301; III ii 58–9, 83–4, 133–9; IV i 56–8; V i 48–50, 98–100, 230–5, 239.

A 'brave new world' is revealed through *discovery* and accompanied by feelings of *wonder, amazement, strangeness* and *rarity.*

Discovery and Wonder:
I ii 14, 198, 306, 406–7, 409–33; II i 6–8, 192–3, 207, 314; II ii throughout; III i 37–48; III ii 131–2; III iii 18–95; IV i 7, 118–24; V i 104–17, 154–62, 170, 178, 181–4, 227–8, 242–4, 261–2, 313–18.

The old world of the past is redeemed by the new world of a hopeful future. The present moment ('now') is a tense turning-point for all the characters. References to *time* are frequent and often related to *fate* or *destiny.*

Time and Fate:
I ii 36–41, 50, 53, 128–9, 159, 178–84, 228, 239–40, 279, 296, 298; II i 12, 175–7, 241–5, III i 22, 40, 95; III iii 53, 68–75, 104–6; IV i 141–2, 144–5, 246, 261–5; V i 1–5, 93, 101, 136, 186, 223, 302.

Prospero is the subject and the agent of destiny, both man and superman. He is grappling with problems which exist in himself as well as in others. His magical powers, like those of an artist (playwright, poet, painter or musician), create (or release) an ideal world from the real one.

Magic:
I ii 1; I ii 24–5, 185–6, 291, 372, 467–74; II i 59–61; III ii 87–91; III iii 17, 52, 82, 88; IV i 35–41, 60–138, 257–60; V i 50–7; Epilogue.

The sound of the sea which surrounds the island beats through the play. We are constantly reminded of its presence.

Sea:
I i 16, 56–9; I ii 1–5, 145–58, 170, 175–7, 210–11, 233–5, 252–3, 301, 375–405, 435–7, 462; II i 59–62, 107–18, 215–23, 232–3, 245–6, II ii 25–7, 42–3, 116–31; III ii 11–14; III iii 8–10, 55–6, 63–4, 71–5, 100–2, IV i 69–70; V i 34–6, 43, 56–7, 79–82, 151–2, 178, 218–25, 270, 314–16.

FURTHER READING

There are several excellent editions of the play available. Frank Kermode's definitive *New Arden* edition (Methuen) has a brilliant introduction and scholarly notes, as does J.H. Walter's thorough *Players' Shakespeare* (Heinemann). Anne Righter's *New Penguin Shakespeare* edition is comparatively thin on notes but has a penetrating and helpful introduction.

One of the best commentaries on the play is by John Dixon Hunt for the Macmillan *Critical Commentaries* series, in which the idea of Prospero as artist is fully developed. The best single volume of past and present criticism is probably D.J. Palmer's selection for the *Casebook* series (Macmillan), which contains such essays as G. Wilson Knight's 'The Shakespearian Superman' in which the characters, imagery and ideas in *The Tempest* are related to other examples in Shakespeare's plays. John Wain has a useful section on the play in *The Living World of Shakespeare* (Pelican), and for the more advanced student, D.G. James's *The Dream of Prospero* (Oxford) should certainly be consulted.

The discussion between L.C. Knights and David Daiches on the play, available as a tape-recording from *Sussex Tapes*, is very well worth hearing.